CAREERS IN

FORENSIC SCIENCE

FORENSIC LA

No Visitors

CAREERS IN

FORENSIC SCIENCE

BY ADAM WOOG

Cavendish
Square

New York

Published in 2014 by Cavendish Square Publishing, LLC
303 Park Avenue South, Suite 1247, New York, NY 10010

Library of Congress Cataloging-in-Publication Data
Woog, Adam, 1953-
Careers in forensic science / Adam Woog.
pages cm. — (Law and order jobs)
Includes bibliographical references.
ISBN 978-1-62712-419-5 (hardcover) ISBN 978-1-62712-420-1 (paperback) ISBN 978-1-62712-421-8 (ebook)
1. Forensic sciences—Vocational guidance. 2. Criminal investigation—Vocational guidance. I. Title.
HV8073.W66 2014
363.25023—dc23

2013030140

EDITORIAL DIRECTOR: DEAN MILLER
ART DIRECTOR: JEFFREY TALBOT
DESIGNER: JOSEPH MACRI
PHOTO RESEARCHER: MARY BETH KAVANAUGH
PRODUCTION MANAGER: JENNIFER RYDER-TALBOT
PRODUCTION EDITOR: ANDREW CODDINGTON

CONTENTS

PRINCE EDWARD ISLAND, CANADA, 1994. THE ROYAL Canadian Mounted Police—Canada's famous Mounties—find a woman's body in a shallow grave. The corpse is that of thirty-two-year-old Shirley Duguay, a mother of five and the former common-law wife of a man named Douglas Beamish.

Beamish, who has a significant criminal record, immediately becomes the prime suspect. But the Mounties have too little evidence to arrest him. The prime piece of evidence is a leather coat found near the scene of the crime. It had belonged to the victim. The coat has bloodstains matching Beamish's blood type, but there's no proof that the blood was Beamish's.

However, police investigators find twenty-seven white hairs on the inside lining of the jacket. Microscopic analysis shows that the hairs are from a cat. One of the Mounties remembers seeing a white cat named Snowball at Beamish's parents' house, where the suspect was living.

The Mounties consider using a branch of science called DNA analysis to pinpoint the cat's identity and link the evidence to their suspect. Running a DNA test on cat hair has never been done, but the Mounties decide the idea is worth

Forensic scientists can help identify unknown murder victims with DNA evidence.

exploring. They send a sample of Snowball's blood and one of the hairs to the Animal Genetics Group at the Laboratory of Genomic Diversity in Frederick, Maryland. One of the lab's geneticists, Marilyn Menotti-Raymond, is an expert on animal DNA. She devises a method to test the samples, and a positive match is made.

But there's still a question: Could Snowball be related to other cats on the island? If so, the hairs could have come from any of them. To make sure, investigators take blood samples of cats from all parts of Prince Edward Island. The samples show that the cats are not alike genetically, which means there's a significant match between Snowball and the hairs. Based largely on this evidence, Beamish is convicted of second-degree murder and sentenced to prison for fifteen years.

The Snowball case set a legal precedent, and DNA evidence

from animals is today widely used around the world. DNA analysis of other animals can now be admitted as evidence in criminal trials as well. Furthermore, an international team of scientists has established an extensive DNA database that will greatly increase the use and reliability of cat hair as evidence. Hair and fur from other animals are part of this database as well.

The database should prove useful because studies have shown that it is virtually impossible for cat owners to avoid having tiny amounts of cat hair on their clothing. These traces can thus become evidence, placing a suspect at the scene of a crime. John Butler, a researcher at the U.S. National Institute of Standards and Technology, affirms this and adds another dimension: "An assailant may unknowingly carry clinging cat hairs from a victim's cat away from the scene of a crime, or hair from the perpetrator's cat may be left at the scene. Either scenario may provide a crucial link and help solve an important case."

The moral of the story? Cat-loving criminals had better take heed because the smallest detail, like a cat hair, can be the smoking gun in a criminal case.

TV IS NOT REAL LIFE

The case of Snowball, the cat that found a murderer, is just one example of how forensic science solves crimes. "Forensic science" is actually a general term encompassing a network of scientific disciplines, such as chemistry, psychology, and engineering. Edward Ricciuti, in his book *Science 101: Forensics*, comments: "Forensics is not about one body of

Crime scene technicians take detailed photographs of every aspect of a crime in order to better understand what happened.

science. Rather, it is about how a host of sciences, and the knowledge accumulated by those who study forensics, are applied to a goal."

That goal is to resolve legal issues. A legal issue might involve an obvious instance of a crime, as in the case of Snowball. But problems that don't necessarily stem from criminal activity also entail legal issues. For example, a forensic scientist's job might be to find out who is at fault in a car accident, discover why a bridge collapsed, identify victims of a natural disaster, or determine what happened to cause an industrial accident in which a worker has been injured.

In recent years, the public's interest in forensics has skyrocketed, fueled especially by TV shows like *Bones*, *Dexter*, and the *CSI* and *Law and Order* franchises. As any forensics expert will tell you, though, *What's on TV is not real forensics.*

The reality is that forensic science, while fascinating, is often messy, tedious, and difficult. Fingerprint dusting can take hours of painstaking work, and when you're done you'll need at least one shower to clean up. Medical examiners don't often look at corpses that appear to be people just sleeping— they see bodies that are decomposed, bloated, or disfigured by gruesome violence. And while a case can end in a quick and satisfying conclusion, that's not always so.

Crime-solving television dramas make forensic science look cool and downright glamorous. The work seems easy, and the results are cut-and-dried. Television, in short, creates an atmosphere of mystery and excitement.

Some of that, certainly, is accurate. Forensics is, indeed, fascinating and challenging work. Essentially, it's the solving of puzzles in order to solve crimes. But don't be fooled—the reality is far from glitz and glamour.

For one thing, labs aren't always shiny, with glass walls and dramatic lighting. They're usually beat-up, windowless rooms with equipment that may be nothing like the high-tech facilities and tools you see on television. And television tends to neglect many essential but time-consuming aspects of police work. Reporter Mara Stine comments in an article in the *Portland* (OR) *Tribune*, " [It's myth that] forensic science databases [on TV] require no significant human action or interpretation to operate, and besides providing evidence match information, [someone must immediately] cough up

Hit television dramas such as the *CSI: Crime Scene Investigation* have significantly increased the public's interest in forensics.

the suspect's photo, rap sheet and last known address. In real life, suspect matches don't just miraculously happen. Hours, days and weeks of work can go into matching a bullet to a gun or DNA to a suspect."

The bottom line: real criminal cases aren't wrapped up as neatly as they are in an hour-long show—even if you add in the minutes that commercials eat up.

WHAT FORENSIC SCIENTISTS DO

Okay, so being a forensic scientist isn't like a TV show. But what is it like? What can you expect if you choose a career in the field?

Well, for one thing, you can count on surprise and variety. Each case will present you with a unique set of challenges.

Each case will have its own special characteristics, as will each piece of evidence. So no two investigations will be alike.

Forensic scientists tend to specialize in particular areas, such as chemistry, weapons analysis, or crime scene investigation. As a result, a single forensic scientist won't conduct evidence investigations, from beginning to end, alone. It's always a team effort. For this reason, generalizing about what these experts do can be difficult.

Nonetheless, some factors are common across all types of forensic science. For example, no matter what branch you choose, your work will typically fall into two basic sections. The first will consist of gathering, identifying, and analyzing physical evidence. The second will involve explaining your findings in a detailed report. This reporting can take one of two forms, or both. You might need to brief your colleagues or law enforcement officials about your conclusions. But you might also give expert **testimony** in court, telling judges, juries, and attorneys what you have found.

Both parts of the process—working with evidence and then explaining your findings—are equally important. You'll be responsible for conducting your work as thoroughly and competently as possible. But it will be equally important for you to present your findings in a clear, unbiased, and balanced way. In other words: all forensic scientists, in both their analysis and reporting, have a commitment to the truth. Henry C. Lee, a distinguished professor of forensic science, writes in his book *Cracking Cases*:

The sole objective of any investigation must be, and always must be, the search for the truth. No matter where the trail of evidence leads and no matter who, if anyone, is ultimately held responsible for the breaking of the law, investigations ultimately get back to that one objective: the truth.

No matter their specialty, forensic scientists are on the front lines of law enforcement. While not all instances of forensic investigation involve dramatic cases, sometimes the work of these scientists proves to be crucial. Sometimes, the conclusions that you'll reach will literally mean the difference between life and death.

THE BIG PICTURE

FORENSIC SCIENCE HAS A LONG HISTORY. HUN-
dreds, perhaps thousands of years have passed since humans
made the first explorations into forensic science. As Professor
Lee comments, "Overall, today's rapidly advancing forensic
technology is grounded on centuries of steady progress in the
field."

The word *forensics* itself is very old. It comes from a Latin
word meaning "of the forum." In ancient Rome, juries of citi-
zens decided criminal cases, and a jury was called a forum.
Over time, "forensics" has come to mean the ways in which
science is used to settle issues concerning the law.

The use of science to solve crimes is likewise very old. The
first known account, a text from thirteenth-century China,
describes such techniques as looking for water in the lungs
of a corpse. The absence of water means that the victim died
of something other than drowning. In one case, the Chinese

While forensics has become more advanced with its study of blood spatter patterns, it can trace its roots back hundreds, if not thousands, of years.

text relates, an imperial investigator solved a murder by first identifying the weapon as a sickle, a tool used to cut grain. He did this by testing different blades on an animal carcass and comparing the wounds they made. He then had all the residents in the area bring their sickles to him. One sickle was singled out because blood on it attracted flies. The investigator confronted the owner of the instrument, who then confessed.

Over the next few hundred years, forensic research grew more sophisticated. For example, in sixteenth-century European surgeons conducted **autopsies** to study how violent death affected internal organs. This knowledge let them make informed guesses about the cause of death. By the mid–1800s, chemists were using reliable methods for identifying poisons.

Meanwhile, courts of law increasingly used forensic evidence. For example, in 1816 a British farmworker was convicted of murdering a servant. The victim had been violently assaulted and drowned. Footprints and an impression of corduroy cloth were found in damp earth near the scene, along with a few grains of wheat. These impressions linked the farmworker to the crime, and he was convicted.

Many familiar methods in modern forensic science were first used in the nineteenth century. For example, in 1835 a British police detective introduced the use of physical analysis to connect a bullet to a murder weapon. Also in Europe during the nineteenth century, methods of identifying fingerprints were developed. The first police crime lab was set up in France in 1910, and by 1924 the United States had one as well. By the mid–twentieth century, the classification of blood types was established, as were **polygraph examinations** and tests to analyze saliva, semen, and other body fluids.

Despite these advances, the legal system was slow to embrace the use of forensic evidence. Author and forensic expert Max M. Houck notes, "Only in the last century has the scientific expert been integrated into the legal arena with a meaningful role."

Today, however, forensic techniques such as fingerprinting and ballistics, along with far more sophisticated methods such as DNA analysis, have become routine elements in legal cases. And the number of organizations that use forensics is enormous. Large agencies, such as the FBI or U.S. Secret Service, typically have their own full-time crime scene investigators and other scientific experts. In other areas, police officers and other law enforcement experts do double duty—that is, they handle forensic work in addition to their other responsibilities.

On the other hand, many forensic scientists are civilian experts who are not employed full-time by a law enforcement agency. Typically, they work for private businesses, consulting and doing lab analysis for a variety of organizations. Normally their business is "on call"—meaning, on an hourly basis as needed.

As a result of this variety, forensic scientists and the labs they work in come in a wide assortment of shapes and sizes, differing in their organization, methods, purposes, and extent. Houck comments:

> It may seem odd, but there is no one structure for the organization of a forensic science laboratory. They vary by jurisdiction (the area for which they are responsible), agency, and history. . . . The analyses and services that a forensic science laboratory provides also [vary], based on the laboratory's budget, personnel and equipment, and the jurisdiction's crime rate.

CRIME SCENE INVESTIGATION

Within the overall field of forensics, specific titles can vary somewhat from agency to agency. For example, crime scene investigators sometimes are known as criminalistics officers, evidence technicians, or forensic investigators.

Crime scene investigators will spend much of their time in the field collecting trace evidence.

More broadly, *criminalist* is sometimes used as a general term for anyone in the field of forensic science. Sometimes the title refers to someone in an agency who performs multiple forensic duties.

Within the broad area of forensic science, there are many subspecialties, each with its own particular area of expertise. Many of these subcategories involve work that is primarily in a laboratory or medical setting, such as a **morgue** or a hospital. But even if you become a lab-based forensic scientist, you might spend a significant amount of your time in the field. This is usually because you may need to see a crime or accident scene or collect data firsthand.

Meanwhile, there is one branch of forensic science that does take place mainly in the field. This is crime scene investigation

(CSI)—the best known of all the specialties within forensic science. Being a crime scene investigator combines knowledge and skills from several different disciplines; it's a mix of science, mathematics, logic, and law.

As a CSI, you'll collect and identify physical evidence that is found, as the name suggests, at a crime scene. This evidence can be almost anything. It might be **trace evidence**, which is just that—tiny bits of evidence—such as a few hairs or fiber threads, a few grass clippings, or a fragment of glass, paper, or wood. It might be a smear of paint or a handful of soil. But even such small bits of evidence can be crucial to a case. In the words of one forensic investigator,

> [T]he most difficult things to collect are, of course, the smallest things. And if offenders have tried to clean up [or if] they're trying to hide the crime scene, offenders will clean it up to the extent that *they* can't see it anymore, and they think that's good enough to get by.

Sometimes, a piece of evidence is much larger than a trace. It might be fairly big, such as a discarded weapon or a car bumper from a hit-and-run accident scene. On occasion, a piece of evidence is very large indeed: computers, cars, and boats are just a few of the items that can be relevant forensic evidence. On its website, the Forensic Sciences Foundation notes: "Physical evidence may be . . . so small that a microscope is needed to see it, or as large as a truck. It may be as subtle as a whiff of

TYPES OF EVIDENCE

Forensic scientists have many specific terms to describe evidence. Here are some of the most common terms.

Circumstantial evidence: evidence that is not a record of direct observation; it consists of information that may lead to conclusions that aren't supported by a confession. Most evidence is actually circumstantial since analysts haven't literally witnessed the crimes they investigate.

Conclusive evidence: evidence that is so convincing that it proves a case.

Conflicting evidence: pieces of evidence that come from different sources and provide contradictory information.

Corroborating evidence: evidence that supports a theory, especially one that has been arrived at on the basis of other evidence.

Demonstrative evidence: evidence that is created after a crime by combining crime scene evidence with information from other sources, such as diagrams of bullet trajectories used for expert witness testimony.

Real evidence: physical, tangible evidence such as blood, hairs, or weapons.

Tainted evidence: evidence that has been altered, deliberately or otherwise, and so is not conclusive or acceptable in court.

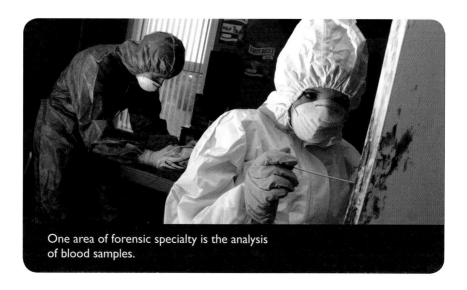

One area of forensic specialty is the analysis of blood samples.

a flammable gas at an arson scene or as obvious as a pool of blood at a homicide scene."

OTHER FORMS OF ANALYSIS

Typically, when a CSI team has finished its work, the evidence collected is passed on to other scientists in one or more specific, specialized areas. Among the many fields of expertise within forensics, for example, is bloodstain pattern analysis (BPA).

Often BPA is done by using photos taken at the scene. If you're a specialist in this field, you'll use principles from disciplines such as physics, biology, and chemistry, as well as knowledge of the three basic types of bloodstain patterns: low-, medium- and high-velocity stains. These tools will allow you to deduce many things about a case: for example, where a victim was before, during, and after an attack; the type of weapon used; the order of events in the attack; and the number of times the victim was assaulted. Often, details about the offender can be discovered as well, such height and left- or right-handedness. Ricciuti comments, "The patterns of bloodstains at a crime scene can tell at least as much about what happened as analysis of the blood itself."

Meanwhile, if a firearm, or evidence of one, is recovered as part of a criminal investigation, the evidence will go to an expert in the science of ballistics. As a ballistics expert, you'll determine identifying details such as the type of gun and caliber of bullet used. Furthermore, you will be able to detect and analyze bullet "fingerprints"—that is, the distinctive marks that are left on bullets after firing. This information can then be used to match a bullet with a particular gun.

A related area of expertise is the field of toolmarks. Tool-marks are any marks that are created by weapons or tools other than firearms. Lengths of steel pipe, rocks, and other blunt objects will leave toolmarks, as will a crowbar used in a robbery or a knife used in an assault. Toolmarks can be very distinctive. For example, a wound from a serrated knife blade looks very different from one made by a smooth blade or a screwdriver.

Meanwhile, another area of forensics focuses on impression evidence. Impression evidence includes footprints, shoeprints, and tire tracks. Less common, and often harder to analyze, are impressions made on material such as fabric, or bite marks on skin or food.

Typically, photos or castings of impression evidence are taken at the scene for later analysis in the lab. The process can yield important information. Take, for example, shoeprints.

From clues like the size of a shoeprint and impressions made in soil or other materials, it's possible to determine with considerable accuracy such individual traits as gender, a limp, or the weight and height of the wearer of the shoe in question. (One rule of thumb is that the length of a person's foot is about 15 percent of his or her height.)

Some forensic scientists focus on investigating possible cases of arson, the deliberate setting of fires. By examining the scene of a fire, arson experts can find evidence that will tell them if the blaze was started on purpose. For example, traces of gasoline or another accelerant may indicate that a fire did not result from a lightning strike or carelessness with matches.

Another familiar branch of forensics is the analysis of fingerprints, the small ridges of skin on the ends of a person's fingers. (Palms and toes also have distinctive ridges, though these are not commonly tested.)

It's possible to use fingerprints for identification because they don't change shape throughout a person's lifetime. They are also unique—that is, each one is different. After a century of analysis and hundreds of millions of recorded prints, no two identical sets of prints have been discovered. Even identical twins have different fingerprints.

DNA ANALYSIS

Another familiar method of identification is the analysis of DNA, the genetic material each person or animal is born with. DNA, which determines individual characteristics, is what makes lions different from cows, or people different from penguins, or you from your best friend. And since people differ in their DNA makeup, analysis of this biological material is a reliable form of identification.

Until recently, DNA analysis was expensive and not very reliable, but today results can be obtained at lower cost and better accuracy. With the most advanced techniques, the chances of an incorrect result can be as low as one in more than a quadrillion (a thousand million million). Compare this to another commonly used technique in criminal investigations: eyewitness accounts. It has been estimated that the probability of an eyewitness account being wrong can be as high as 50 percent.

The best-known use of DNA analysis is to identify offenders and victims during a criminal investigation. But as a DNA analyst, you'll undoubtedly work on cases of many other kinds as well. For example, DNA can help identify victims of natural disasters and other catastrophes. It can also have an impact on legal cases in a number of other ways: by establishing blood family relationships, for instance, or by confirming the presence of organic pollutants in the environment or in food supplies.

The analysis of DNA evidence has become increasingly accurate and less expensive to obtain.

The technology associated with DNA analysis can even

JURIES, TV, AND REAL LIFE

Judges and attorneys have a phrase for it: the CSI effect. It's noted when remarks by people on juries indicate that they have unrealistic expectations about forensic evidence and tests. They've watched the TV shows, and they think they know what needs to be done.

It's gotten so bad in recent years, some say, that scientists who take the stand to give testimony need to spend fifteen or twenty minutes explaining why the evidence isn't going to be presented the way it is on TV. There's even a subspecialty to address the CSI effect—many attorneys use "negative witnesses," experts whose only job is to explain why some forensic work wasn't done.

The truth is that in most cases law enforcement agencies simply don't have the resources or budgets for high-tech equipment and analysis. Agencies that do, such as the FBI, typically have huge backlogs and waiting periods for forensic work to be completed.

Some courts have gone so far as to issue specific instructions to juries. For example, the Ohio Bar Association recommends that judges tell juries the following:

> The effort to exclude misleading outside influences [and] information also puts a limit on getting legal information from television entertainment. This would apply to popular TV shows such as *Law and Order*, *Boston Legal*, *Judge Judy*, older shows like *L.A. Law*, *Perry Mason*, or *Matlock*, and any other fictional show dealing with the legal system. In addition, this would apply to shows such as *CSI* and *NCIS*, which present the use of scientific procedures to resolve criminal investigations. These and other similar shows may leave you with an improper preconceived idea about the legal system.
>
> As far as this case is concerned, you are not prohibited from watching such shows. However, there are many reasons why you cannot rely on TV legal programs, including the fact that these shows: (1) are not subject to the rules of evidence and legal safeguards that apply in this courtroom, and (2) are works of fiction that present unrealistic situations for dramatic effect. While entertaining, TV legal dramas condense, distort, or even ignore many procedures that take place in real cases and real courtrooms. No matter how convincing they try to be, these shows simply cannot depict the reality of an actual trial or investigation. You must put aside anything you think you know about the legal system that you saw on TV.

Source:"The CSI Effect," Forensicscience.org,
www.forensicscience.net/the-csi-effect

Analysis of skeletons can provide clues to crimes that are decades old.

be used to protect against fraud. For example, synthetic DNA tags have been attached to Super Bowl footballs and souvenirs from Olympic games. (This synthetic DNA is similar to the material scientists have created to perform tasks such as genetically modifying food.) By using a special laser to identify these tags, forensic analysts can eliminate the chance of fraud in the lucrative sports memorabilia trade.

FORENSIC TOXICOLOGY, ODONTOLOGY, AND PATHOLOGY

Forensic scientists called toxicologists are specialists in the study of poisons and harmful chemicals and drugs. This field combines aspects of chemistry and medicine. Sometimes forensic toxicologists are called in to determine if a death was the result of drug or alcohol abuse, or if substance abuse was a factor in the commission of a crime. Some cases involve analyzing suspicious substances that may be harmful, such as the envelopes containing deadly anthrax spores that were mailed to people and news organizations after the 9/11 terrorist attacks. And some forensic toxicologists work for labs that conduct drug tests for workplace employees or athletes.

Forensic pathology and forensic odontology are related to the field of forensic toxicology. Pathology is the study of disease, and a forensic pathologist (also called a medical examiner) is a physician who investigates sudden, unexpected, and/or violent deaths. (Coroners have somewhat related jobs, although coroners are not necessarily physicians.)

Forensic odontology is the science of identifying people through dental records and inspection of teeth. In addition to aiding criminal investigations, both forensic pathology and forensic odontology can help in such tasks as identifying bodies in the wake of natural disasters, bombings, or other catastrophes. Even a few teeth can be enough to provide vital clues to a victim's identity, or a single bite mark can help in identifying a criminal.

FORENSIC ANTHROPOLOGY AND
FACIAL RECONSTRUCTION

Anthropology, broadly speaking, is the study of humans and their cultures. Forensic anthropology combines anthropology with osteology, the study of bones. Forensic anthropologists study human remains to determine a victim's physical characteristics, typically to identify them and determine the cause of death. Old bones can reveal a lot of information, Ricciuti notes

With facial reconstruction technology, forensic scientists can extrapolate an individual's appearance from her skull.

"A pile of bones found in the basement of an old building or in a shallow grave may look like a gruesome, jumbled mess to the average person, but to a forensic anthropologist it represents reading material of a sort."

Often, bodies or skeletons are recovered that are unrecognizable due to decomposition, burns, or trauma (severe damage). Even so, forensic anthropologists can use a variety of techniques to "read" these remains and determine such characteristics as age, sex, size, ethnicity, height, occupation, and overall health at the time of death. The first step, of course, is to see if the remains are human. Sometimes, what people think are human bones turn out to be those of animals. The next step is to closely examine all the remains that have been recovered to discover clues about the victim. Was it an accidental death? Natural causes? Homicide? Suicide?

If you choose to become a forensic anthropologist, your work will often be connected to solving crimes. This is not always so, however. For example, you might be called on to help identify victims of a disaster such as a plane crash, an explosion, or a fire. And sometimes a forensic anthropologist's work involves forming opinions about very old bones. In fact, scientists have been able to discover the probable cause of death of ancient Egyptian pharaohs.

Forensic anthropology is one of the most rare specialties within the scope of forensic science. This is primarily because relatively few cases require these skills. As a result, most forensic anthropologists teach or do research at universities, acting as consultants on a part-time basis. Aaron Elkins, a police consultant and the author of many mystery novels featuring forensic anthropologist Gideon Oliver, comments

> The only full-time [practitioners] I know about work either for mass-disaster agencies or for a U.S. Army skeletal identification outfit in Hawaii that looks into things wherever American remains from WWII, Korea, or Vietnam are discovered.
>
> Maybe one out of fifty forensic pathologists is a full-timer. . . . There just aren't enough skeletons turning up in the woods to give many people full-time work. I've been the consulting forensic anthropologist for the Clallam County [Washington] Sheriff's Department for maybe four years . . . and I've only had two cases to

WHAT FORENSIC ANTHROPOLOGISTS DO

In addition to writing many mystery novels starring forensic anthropologist Gideon "The Bone Detective" Oliver, Aaron Elkins is also a consultant to the Clallam County Sheriff's Department in Washington. Here, he reflects on what a forensic anthropologist does.

Imagine that you're a homicide detective. Your lieutenant calls you in and tells you that a call just came in from a hunter out in the woods, who has just come across a few scattered bones, and they look suspiciously to him as if they might be human. "Get out there right now and have a look," the lieutenant tells you.

Well, if you're like most police officers, you couldn't tell a tibia from a humerus, or a goat femur from a human fibula in a handful of bones. So, you call in the department's consulting forensic anthropologist, whose expertise in human skeletal remains makes him or her your best asset in anything involving bones.

First, he or she can tell you right off if the remains are or aren't human. And if they are—depending on what bones have been found and what their condition is—he or she might be able to tell you a lot of things about them that can help identify just whose bones they are: the person's age, sex, race, height, and general physique, plus signs of old injuries, diseases, and anatomical peculiarities, plus how long the bones have been out there. He or she might also very well be able to tell you what the cause of death was, and even what the person did for a living.

A forensic anthropologist's work is extremely rewarding. We think of ourselves as the last voice to speak on behalf of the dead, who would otherwise lie unknown and (in the case of murder) unavenged.

And then there are the little oddities and surprises that come along to make life interesting. Here's an example: The skeleton of a man who'd been missing for many years finally turned up in a storage unit. His wife was one of the suspects, but the case was never resolved.

The remains were turned over to her (they always go back to the family in the end) and she donated them to a forensics lab at the local college—on condition that she could come and visit her skeletonized spouse whenever she felt the need to "commune" with him. A couple of years later, new evidence came to light and the wife was tried for his murder and convicted. When she was asked afterward what the "communing" was all about, her answer was: "I just liked to come and make sure the !!&*!!%% was really dead." It's not every occupation that can provide you with educational and uplifting experiences like that.

Source: e-mail to author, August 21, 2011.

work on, both of which were simply unresolved ones from earlier years.

Allied to forensic anthropology is the field of forensic facial reconstruction. As the name implies, specialists use the existing remains of a skull to create a model of how that person's face might have looked. A facial reconstructionist is typically requested when investigators need to identify an unknown victim. By using evidence such as skulls (or even skull fragments), reconstruction professionals are able to build up a close approximation of a victim's features. The result might take the form of hand-made sketches, clay sculptures, or computer-generated images.

In many ways, facial reconstruction is as much art as science. It combines the creative and imaginative aspects of the visual arts with a variety of scientific disciplines, including anatomy and anthropology. So if you have an artistic bent, this might be a good choice for you.

FORENSIC PSYCHOLOGY

Crime scene investigation, DNA and fingerprint analysis, toxicology, pathology, forensic anthropology, and related branches of forensic science concentrate on evidence that is primarily physical. Forensic psychology is something else entirely. Its focus is on an intangible quality: mental health as it applies to legal questions.

Perhaps the most familiar form of forensic psychology is profiling, or the process of seeking out patterns in psychological makeup. Profiling can give investigators insights into the behavior, motives, and backgrounds of criminals—and thus, in some cases, allow experts to predict what characteristics a fugitive will have.

Profiling is a highly specialized skill, and only a handful of experts in the United States have the necessary background of education and experience. The popular image of this field, as portrayed on TV and elsewhere, indicates that forensic psychologists deal mainly with creating profiles of serial killers or sitting down with criminals to find out what's in their heads. However, forensic psychologists do much more. All of their work is important, but it is not necessarily glamorous. For example, they painstakingly analyze huge amounts of data that has been collected from previous cases. This helps them find patterns of behavior. Such aspects of the job are quite different from the popular image of a forensic psychologist's work.

Profiling is far from the only area of forensic psychology, however; there are many other aspects to the field. If you choose to go into the field of forensic psychology, you could work in a prison, a legal firm, a private company, or in a school. You might consult with law enforcement agencies and lawyers in cases involving child custody disputes or during investigations of allegations of child abuse. In such situations, you would assess the mental health of the children and adults involved. Other typical tasks for forensic psychologists include taking part in competency hearings (in which a suspect's mental health is assessed to see if he or she is fit to stand trial) or parole hearings (to see if convicts should be allowed to leave prison before completing their terms).

PROFILING THE GREEN RIVER KILLER

The Green River Killer terrorized Washington State in the 1980s and 1990s with a string of gruesome murders of women. The story of his capture demonstrates how detectives tracked him down by means of psychological profiling. Based on the evidence found at the scenes of certain crimes, a team of FBI behavioral psychologists led by Special Agent John Douglas compiled a twelve-page profile of the killer.

After more than twenty years of investigation, a man named Gary Leon Ridgway was arrested on the suspicion of four murders. A large part of the success of the investigation that led to his detention resulted from the profiling work.

Among the many predictions the FBI made were suggestions that the killer was probably white, male, well organized, careful, eager to help the police in their investigations, and likely to kill again. As these general characteristics suggest, profiling is not an exact science. In fact, the FBI also predicted that the killer was probably an outdoorsman and had difficulty connecting emotionally with people, neither of which proved to be the case.

As part of a plea bargain to avoid the death penalty, Ridgway later confessed to forty-eight murders and led investigators to the hidden remains of some of his victims. He is now serving a life sentence without parole.

WHAT FORENSIC PSYCHOLOGISTS
NEED TO KNOW

Forensic psychology, like other kinds of forensic science, is an extremely complex subject and requires years of study in highly specialized areas. Here is an abbreviated list some of the things you'll need to have under your belt.

- Ability to conduct diagnostic mental health examinations on, and provide treatment to, mentally ill and sometimes dangerous individuals
- Ability to conduct psychological assessments to determine criminal responsibility for illegal acts
- Ability to conduct research, prepare reports, and educate others on matters of forensic psychology
- Ability to prepare concise reports detailing findings and conclusions of psychological evaluations
- Ability to provide expert testimony
- Ability to provide testimony relative to the psychological state of individuals and their ability to stand trial
- Knowledge of emotional and social, psychological, and environmental problems
- Knowledge of techniques for observing and assessing behavior
- Knowledge of techniques of conducting objective interviews

Adapted from the Michigan Civil Service Commission's job specifications for Forensic Psychologist, www.michigan.gov/documents/ForensicPsychologist_12008_7.pdf

QUESTIONED-DOCUMENT EXAMINATION
AND DIGITAL FORENSICS

Another important branch of forensics is devoted to the science of examining questioned documents. The definition of "questioned document" can be very broad. Typically, the phrase refers to a suspicious document such as a will that might have been forged, a check someone thinks has been altered, or money a citizen believes to be counterfeit. But the term can also be used in a much broader sense. As a questioned-document specialist, you might examine graffiti on a wall (because the markings may be potential evidence) or a trademark improperly used on consumer goods (which would indicate fraud).

Questioned-document analysis is often used in the investigation of **white-collar crimes** such as identity theft, fraud, and counterfeiting. However, it is used in many other situations as well. For example, analysis may prove that a document alleged to be a suicide note was forged, thus opening up the possibility that the dead person, supposedly the author of the note, was murdered.

White-collar crime is also the focus of another branch of forensics: digital forensics. Digital forensics (also called computer forensics) is used in solving crimes by means of retrieving, analyzing, and/or using digital information such as data found in computer hard drives, cell phones, cameras, personal digital assistants, and other devices.

Within digital forensics, there are many even more highly focused fields. For example, image enhancement specialists are experts in digitally improving the clarity of a photo or confirming its authenticity. Digital audio scientists, meanwhile, focus on such tasks as identifying voices on recordings, cleaning up recordings to make them more intelligible, authenticating transcripts of conversations, and confirming that no one has tampered with a recording.

SUPPORT POSITIONS

Specialized positions in forensics are reserved for highly trained scientists with years of experience and education. However, these jobs are by no means the only ones available to you in the field of forensic science. In particular, forensic scientists, like other professionals, need reliable teams to assist and support them. Employment in forensic science, in any capacity, is part of a team effort, since no single person can do it all. Whether support employees work for law enforcement agencies, private labs, or elsewhere, they are vital in making sure that things run smoothly for the senior scientists in the agency.

In some cases, support positions in a forensics lab are like the jobs you would find in any business: office managers, secretaries, administrators, accountants, storage and management specialists, and security officers. In addition, labs always have a need for employees in more technical positions such as database management and record keeping, computer security, and instrument installation, calibration, and maintenance.

Many members of a support staff are essentially assistants to senior scientists. Even if you have had years of training and education in a particular area such as toxicology, it's likely that your first job will be as an assistant. As you would expect, this is because you will need experience as well as a sound educational background before you can move into a position with greater responsibility, more prestige, and a higher salary.

LEARNING MORE

Clearly, there are many aspects to having a career in forensic science—and many paths to take. There are a number of ways to find out more to help you decide which of these paths you'd like to take.

A couple of good places to start are the websites of two prominent professional organizations: the American Academy of Forensic Sciences (AAFS): www.aafs.org and the American Forensic Association: www.americanforensics.org. You might also want to look at the websites of the many organizations devoted to particular subspecialties of forensic science. If you are interested in working for a federal agency, the U.S. government's central job site, www.usajobs.opm.gov, has information about forensic science employment within its various agencies.

Furthermore, you can contact a local law enforcement agency. Recruiters for these agencies will always be interested in talking with you about your possible career options.

To varying degrees, these sites will give you general information as well as specifics, such as how to connect with working professionals in your area or see listings of current job openings. Looking at these sites will give you an idea of where you'd like to go on your career path. And then you can start getting more specific about planning your education.

WHAT IT TAKES

SO WHAT DOES IT TAKE TO BE A FORENSIC SCIENTIST? Well, obviously, a good education in science and a strong interest in law enforcement. But there's more to it than that. A number of personality traits and characteristics will help you be an effective and competent forensic scientist.

PERSONAL CHARACTERISTICS

Generally speaking, one of the things you'll need is a strong stomach. In many branches of forensic science, you'll be observing, collecting, and analyzing some really gruesome materials. This should go without saying, since a crime scene technician's primary workplace is often a scene of violence and death.

Even a specialist who works mostly in a laboratory setting, somewhat removed from the "real world," will often have grisly work like that of medical examiners, who dissect bodies to

Before deciding that a career in forensics is right for you, consider whether you'd be able to handle working in gruesome crime scene settings.

look for clues. Does the prospect of dealing with the grim physical aftermath of crime make you queasy? If so, then forensic science may not be the field for you. On the other hand, if the prospect of such a nontraditional workplace doesn't bother you, then forensic science might be a great match for you.

Another crucial personal characteristic is an aptitude for precision. No matter what branch of forensic science you choose, you will first and foremost be a scientist—and forensics is as rigorously precise as any other scientific field. So you'll need to have a detail-oriented mindset, as well as accurate and meticulous work habits. After all, a slip-up could have profound consequences. A sloppy job, the misreading of data, or an incorrect statement in court could result in unlawful arrest, a mistrial, a criminal who escapes conviction to break the law again, or the conviction of an innocent person.

A meticulous frame of mind will help you in a number of ways on the job. For example, it will help you maintain an unbroken **chain of custody** (also called a chain of evidence). A chain of custody is a complete record of how a piece of evidence is handled. Various security measures, such as signatures of everyone who handles the evidence, along with verification of each person's identification, are part of this process. A well-maintained chain helps ensure that your results will be accurate because the process makes it difficult to tamper with or accidentally contaminate evidence.

On the other hand, you'll also have to be comfortable with a certain level of ambiguity. That is, you will sometimes have to accept that your test results are uncertain or inconclusive. Sometimes there is conflicting data, or just not enough of it, and you won't be able to state a conclusion with complete certainty. In other words, even if you are competent and meticulous and do your job to the best of your ability, you won't always have all the answers.

Another important trait for a forensic scientist is the ability to switch gears abruptly between measured patience and speed. Would you be able to stick to a task if months, or even years, were needed to find a solution? Conversely, do you have what it takes to work well under pressure when faced with a time-sensitive task?

Furthermore, forensics requires a certain creative flair, as well as imagination and curiosity. This is because not every case will be cut and dried, and not every clue will be obvious. In this respect, solving a criminal case is like putting together a puzzle. It will take a powerful streak of curiosity and perception for you to see patterns or solutions among seemingly unconnected pieces of evidence. One crime scene investigator comments: "You have to be very adaptive and flexible. You can't walk in and say, 'It happened this way.' You weren't there when it happened. It might *seem* like it happened this way, but it can be completely different."

In addition to creativity and curiosity, some areas of forensic science require artistic skill. For example, facial reconstruction experts need excellent drawing, sculpting, and computer graphics abilities. If that's a career you're interested in, you'll also need to be creative in your use of clay and other materials such as wigs and artificial eyes. Imagination is also required for the job, since often you won't know the identity of the person whose face you're reconstructing.

Another important personal trait for a forensic scientist to have is an ability and willingness to work hard. Ask yourself: Am I able to commit myself to a task? Do I have a strong work ethic? Am I willing and able to put in long hours, sometimes at odd times or without having breaks for regular meals, to complete a job?

Also, are you prepared to travel as part of your work? Depending on your specialty and the specifics of a case, you might work more or less all the time in one environment. On the other hand, you may need to travel regularly. Sometimes your trips will be to present your findings to groups, such as conferences, groups of law enforcement officers, or juries in court cases. At other times, you may be asked to travel to remote or rugged environments so that you can collect evidence for later analysis or take care of other tasks.

MORE CHARACTERISTICS AND PRACTICAL CONSIDERATIONS

On top of all the personal characteristics, you will need good communication skills. A large part of your time as a forensic scientist will be spent writing reports and presenting your conclusions orally to members of the **lay public**. It is unlikely that they will have had your scientific training, so they will not be familiar with technical terms. Will you be able to explain things to them in simple, understandable, and accurate ways? Furthermore, do you have the ability to connect well with other people on a personal basis? This will be a particularly strong asset to have when you testify in court. An expert witness who is open and friendly will hold the attention of a jury much more easily than a witness who is cold and clinical.

There are also questions to ask yourself about your preference regarding potential colleagues. As a forensic scientist, on occasion you'll no doubt spend long hours on your own. For example, you might need to work by yourself on an autopsy or an analysis of chemicals found at the scene of a crime. So you should ask yourself: Am I motivated enough to work well solo?

At the same time, forensics is a collaborative process. You'll frequently be part of a close-knit group of people. Do you work well with others in a team situation? Would you be comfortable leading a group and giving orders? And would the opposite also be true—will you do well at following someone else's leadership?

Related to the ability to work collaboratively is the requirement to deal with people, besides your colleagues, who are connected with a case. Forensic scientists work in the real world, not in a vacuum. In your job you may encounter a wide variety of people, from prisoners and the mentally ill to family members, witnesses, and other individuals connected with a case. If you have to meet with the grieving, distraught members of a victim's family, a high degree of compassion, sensitivity, and understanding will be essential.

There are also various other practical considerations. Your overall physical fitness will be important. Also, in the majority of forensic work, you will need to have good eyesight (perhaps with glasses or contacts) to be able to spot clues at a crime scene or use a microscope effectively to examine tiny bits of evidence. Like poor eyesight, color blindness will make your work more difficult, and in some cases perhaps impossible. Also in the vein of practical considerations, a valid driver's license and basic computer skills are common requirements for both specialized work and support positions.

Furthermore, you will need a clean record when it comes to arrests and drug use. For obvious reasons, no law enforcement agency or private lab is going to hire you if your personal history indicates that you might be at high risk for **corruption**, or if your work could be affected by drug use.

There will be several components to checking your past record. For one thing, it's likely that you'll be asked to take a polygraph (often called "lie detector") exam. You'll also undergo a thorough background check that will cover your finances, personal character, and other matters. If you have an arrest record other than minor traffic citations, your chances of being hired will be dramatically lower. Hiring decisions often are made on a case-by-case basis, however. A history of prior drug use also is not an automatic deal breaker. As for ongoing drug use, agencies and labs generally require random, periodic testing of their employees.

MAKING A PLAN

If you've considered all the personal characteristics needed to be a good forensic scientist, and you think you have what it takes, the next step is to create a plan for the future. Simply put, it's never too early to start preparing.

Perhaps the most important thing you can do is to take as many science and math classes as you can. These should include a thorough grounding in at least the basics of biology, chemistry, physics, computer science, and math. And you'll need more than theoretical classroom learning—it's also important to get as much hands-on time with microscopes and other instruments as possible.

Writing well is another important skill. The reports you will prepare must be clear, concise, well organized, and easily understood by non-experts. So a key part of your plan should be to constantly improve your writing skills, even if you already write well. Developing the habit of taking detailed notes in all your classes will help you prepare for working efficiently down the road.

A related communications skill is the ability to articulate your opinions and findings in front of a group. You'll have a special need for these verbal skills in the courtroom, because it will be important for you to impress judges and juries with your confidence, knowledge, and clarity of speech. It's therefore an excellent idea to work on your public speaking skills. You might be able to do this by joining your school's debate team or drama club.

Furthermore, you can start adding to your overall knowledge of forensics by looking at newspapers, periodicals, and websites for articles that can keep you up to date on topics related to forensics. A cautionary note: In this and any other research, make sure that sources you find on the Internet—or elsewhere, for that matter—are reputable and trustworthy. To ensure accuracy, always go to reputable Internet sites such as those maintained by universities, government agencies, legitimate news sources, or professional organizations.

Sometimes, your high school studies can be even more specific. If you're lucky, your school will have science classes with units specifically devoted to forensic science. And if you're really lucky, your school will offer yearlong classes on the subject. Forensics has become an increasingly popular subject, thanks to the high level of interest among students. According to a poll taken by the National Science Teachers Association, 75 percent of the nation's school districts said that they use forensic investigation techniques to teach science in the classroom, and about 25 percent had entire classes devoted to the subject.

Scott Rubins is an example of a science teacher who has designed entire classes devoted to forensics. It's one of the most popular classes in his school, New Rochelle High School in New Rochelle, New York. As *New York Times* science

Handling live maggots may be disgusting for some, but it's part of the job for forensic specialists.

writer Natalie Angier comments, "Since the program [at New Rochelle High] was started . . . demand has waxed so strong that today the school offers seven different forensic classes, three of them so advanced that the students receive college credits."

Rubins doesn't pull his punches when it comes to the grisly subjects his students examine. Things do get a little messy at times. However, the teacher has a strict rule in his classroom: no one is allowed to express disgust, at least out loud. Not that there's much danger of that—any student who enrolls in Rubins's classes needs to be eager to examine dead, decaying animals and other items that have a high yuck factor. In Angier's *New York Times* article, one senior at New Rochelle commented, "I love this class! Where else do you get the chance to hold maggots?"

INTERNSHIPS

Even if your school doesn't offer a class that lets you hold maggots, there are other ways to learn about forensics during your high school career. For example, you may be able to "shadow" scientists in a laboratory near you, spending a day or a week observing them as they go about their work. You can find these local labs in a number of ways, such as by contacting law enforcement agencies near you. Another good resource is the website of the American Academy of Forensic Sciences (AAFS): www.aafs.org.

An excellent way to get a taste of what forensic scientists do on a daily basis is to attend a summer workshop designed for high school students. There are a number of such programs around the country. For example, one of these "forensic camps" is sponsored by Georgetown University in Washington, D.C. It's a weeklong course of study during which students learn the basics of forensic science, including such subjects as computer forensics, ballistics, and bloodstain pattern analysis.

If you're interested, some summer workshops for high school students go into greater depth. One such camp is held at Syracuse University in Syracuse, New York. This six-week program will have you learning in the classroom as well as in the field as part of a team that gathers evidence from a simulated crime scene. Among the topics covered at Syracuse are DNA, blood, and hair analysis; microscopic investigations, forensic psychology, toxicology, fingerprints, and arson investigation.

When you become a college student, you will find many other opportunities for hands-on experience. One way is to become an intern in a forensic science lab. Across the country, a number of organizations—university labs, law enforcement labs, and facilities in the private sector—offer such programs. Some internships are paid positions, while others are staffed by volunteers.

Typically, internships are set up to accommodate the schedule of your regular classes. Some are designed for students who are already majoring in a related field, while others are available to a more general student population. College internships are often excellent bridges between school and work, since you will not only gain experience, you will be personally known by the staff of the agency where you are interning.

Volunteering in other ways, outside the realm of government or private labs, can provide you with valuable experience as well. Laura Sheahan, a scientist who now works for an organization that promotes science education, notes:

> Becoming involved in activities outside of . . . school can also be helpful if you are considering a career [in science]. During my last two years of school I volunteered at the Carnegie Science Museum in Pittsburgh to help a team of academics and local government officials devise a plan to reform math and science education in southwestern Pennsylvania. It was a fun and rewarding endeavor [and may] significantly impact the future of science education in the region.

There's still another way you can get an idea of what it would be like to have a career in forensic science. You can join the Young

Forensic Scientists Forum (YFSF). This is a group sponsored by the American Academy of Forensic Sciences (AAFS). According to the YFSF website, the organization is "dedicated to the education, enrichment and development of emerging forensic scientists and future leaders of the field."

One of the organization's activities is to sponsor meetings and educational sessions for students at its conferences. The AAFS also publishes a newsletter especially for students, provides a reduced-rate subscription to its regular periodical, and maintains a website and informational databases. Furthermore, it has a program that matches students with forensic scientists drawn from all sections of the AAFS. Through it, scientists can mentor students through the process of planning a career in the field.

To learn more about the Young Forensic Scientists Forum, visit the organization's website: http://yfsf.aafs.org.

WRITING A RÉSUMÉ

If you apply to the YFSF or a summer program or internship, you will need to write a résumé. (The same is true, of course, when it comes time to apply for a job, in forensics or any other field.) A good résumé will give an organization's recruiters details about your qualifications and experience—in other words, it will say why you would be a good fit. A good place to find help in putting your résumé together is your school's career center.

Your résumé should be accompanied by a concise cover letter. Write perhaps three or four paragraphs; never put more than will fit on a single page. The idea is to give the reader as much information as possible in a small space. Ideally, a cover

When applying for a forensics position (or any job), a well-written résumé can distinguish you from the other candidates.

letter will be addressed to the person in charge of hiring. For that reason, it's a good idea to try to find out the name of the person who will be reading your submission. It's much better to be able to start with "Dear . . . " than with a more impersonal phrase such as "To whom it may concern. . . . "

The cover letter is your opportunity to introduce yourself. It should summarize the points that you'll detail in your résumé. It should also show your enthusiasm and express why you think you are the right person for the job. Don't be afraid to brag a little—this is one time when it's appropriate. On the other hand, avoid sounding arrogant or self-focused. And don't lie! You're sure to be caught at some point.

End your cover letter with a few words thanking the recipient for taking time to consider you, and sign off by saying that you hope to have a chance to speak in person soon. Then you can attach your résumé as a separate document. Typically, a résumé will include the following:

- Contact information. Complete and current contact information is essential to allow a potential employer to be able to reach you easily.
- Education and training. This will include the names of the schools you attended and the dates, your grade point averages, any awards you might have won, and so on.
- Work experience and other experience. Start with the most recent experience and work backward. Again, be sure to provide details, especially the length of your employment or volunteer stint, the names and companies or groups you worked for, and short summaries of your responsibilities there.
- Any other qualifications. Here, you should mention any accomplishments that might make your job application stand out. These might be membership in a club, community service, awards, internships, or published articles.
- References. State that these will be available on request.
- Finally, remember that neatness counts! Just like a job in forensic science, your cover letter and résumé need to be well written and meticulously prepared, showing the detail orientation employers value. Incorrect spelling or bad grammar, typographical mistakes, or other slip-ups are clearly not going to do you any good.

Knowing how to prepare a good résumé will also help you in your next step toward a career in forensics: choosing the right school to attend.

THREE

HIGHER EDUCATION AND TRAINING

WHEN IT COMES TIME TO START LOOKING AHEAD to your post high school education, there are a number of important points to consider. First, look for a school that features a strong science program. Read the course descriptions in college catalogs thoroughly; if possible, visit the schools that interest you. This will help you make sure that the school you finally choose will offer classes that can provide the depth of study you'll need.

The school of your choice doesn't necessarily have to have a specific emphasis on forensic science. In fact, some experts will tell you that a background in a more general field of science, such as chemistry or physics, is in some ways better. One reason for this is that it will give you more flexibility in the job market. So, if you decide to move out of the forensics field, you'll stand a better chance of landing a job elsewhere if you have a more general degree. Dale Nute, a professor at Florida State University's School of Criminology and Criminal Justice, expands on this point:

> If the job market for forensic scientists is weak, you will have trouble getting a job with a chemical firm with a forensic science degree. On the other hand, if you have a traditional chemistry degree, you can always get a job in a crime laboratory if they are available. And, if none are available, you are more likely to get a decent job somewhere and can then move into a forensic science career when crime laboratory jobs are more plentiful.

CHOOSING A SCHOOL

The school you choose might be a university, a community or career college, or an online school. Your decision will depend on several factors. For one thing, some schools offering criminal justice programs don't focus on forensics. For example the University of Florida and the University of Maryland operate respected criminal justice programs. However, they are quite different. Florida has an extensive forensic science department, while Maryland focuses on research, not on forensic science.

You'll have a distinct advantage if you can get a four-year bachelor of arts (BA) or bachelor of science (BS) degree. (These are also called undergraduate degrees.) A bachelor's-level degree will let you start out with a better and more challenging job than you will be eligible for with an associate of arts (AA) degree from a community, vocational, or online college.

Getting an AA degree is likely the way to go if your grades aren't good enough to get you into a four-year school, or if you aren't sure that you are ready for classes on a university campus. It typically takes two years to earn an AA degree from a community, online, or career (vocational) college.

With an AA degree in hand, you will be qualified for one of several entry-level jobs. Among these is a position such as a forensic science specialist (an assistant to a senior scientist). An entry-level job like this is an excellent stepping-stone toward a higher position. For one thing, you'll be among the first to know when job positions become available in your workplace. The lab personnel will already know you, your educational background, and your capabilities. Also, labs often will encourage employees to further their education while on the job. This encouragement can take on a variety of forms, such as giving you time off to attend seminars or even paying your tuition to earn a more advanced degree.

Meanwhile, studying for a forensic degree online is becoming more popular. This option has both advantages and disadvantages. One big downside is that you won't have opportunities to get hands-on experience in labs (unless you can arrange to do so, perhaps as an intern, in a lab near you). Also, you won't experience the type of give-and-take learning that comes from attending classes with other students on a physical campus.

On the other hand, an online course of study allows you to learn at your own pace and watch videos of lectures as many times as you like, concentrating on what's being taught rather than having to hastily make notes in class. Furthermore, online learning is good for people who, because of jobs, family obligations, or other commitments, can't be in classes at a set time each day or week. Furthermore, online schools may be a good solution if there isn't an appropriate bricks-and-mortar school near your home and you are unable to relocate.

No matter which type of school you choose, it's important to make sure that it is properly accredited. Law enforcement agencies, private companies, and other organizations will be unlikely to hire you if you have not graduated from a properly **accredited school**.

When you have narrowed your choices to a few possibilities, it's time to start looking at specifics. By visiting these schools, auditing a class, or scheduling a call with your chosen program's department head, you can find much of the information you need. Among the questions you should try to answer are: What is the program's emphasis? Does it stress theoretical or practical knowledge, or both? Are its facilities up-to-date? Does the school have small class sizes? (If they're small, you'll have more individual attention from instructors and time with lab equipment.) And is the school associated with a law enforcement agency or other organization that can provide real-life experience as part of your training?

DEGREES IN FORENSIC SCIENCE

Some colleges offer a specific undergraduate degree in forensic science. Typically, these combine a traditional science degree (such as chemistry or biology) with classes covering forensics and criminal justice. One obvious benefit of a degree in forensic science is that you'll know you've taken all the coursework needed for an entry-level job after graduation.

Another good thing about a forensics degree is that this course of study can give you a chance to be part of a working forensics lab, typically as an intern at an outside lab or by doing research in the university's forensic facilities. Having honed your hands-on skills in this way will be a real advantage when you look for work—employers like to see that you have some real-life experience as well as academic training.

If you're interested in a specific program for forensic science, there are several ways to find out about schools that offer them. Once again, the American Academy of Forensic Science's website can help: www.aafs.org. The AAFS maintains an up-to-date list of accredited schools offering these programs, which as of 2011 included:

Many colleges offer classes in forensics to help prepare you for your career.

- Cedar Crest College, Allentown, PA
- City University of New York, John Jay College of Criminal Justice, New York City, NY
- Eastern Kentucky University, Richmond, KY
- Florida International University, Miami, FL
- Indiana University, Bloomington, IN
- Metropolitan State College of Denver, Denver, CO
- Ohio University, Athens, OH
- Pennsylvania State University, Eberly College of Science, University Park, PA
- Purdue University, West Lafayette, IN
- State University of New York/Albany, Albany, NY
- University of Mississippi, Oxford, MS
- University of New Haven, New Haven, CT
- University of North Texas, Denton, TX
- Virginia Commonwealth University, Richmond, VA
- West Virginia University, Morgantown, WV

After you decide on a school, you'll obviously need to apply—a situation in which your résumé-writing skills will come in very handy. Talk to your family or school counselors to figure out the best time for you to start the application process. If all goes well, you'll be accepted by the school of your choice, and you'll be ready to take the next step toward becoming a forensic scientist: going to college.

COLLEGE STUDIES

No matter what school you choose, the exact makeup of your

course of study will depend on many things. You'll have a number of options, which in turn will vary according to your interests and the program's requirements. For example, you can major in a one of the so-called hard sciences—such as chemistry or physics—with a minor in forensics. Or you could major in a science and minor in criminal justice and **criminology**. Or you could do a double major in information technology and forensic sciences. In any case, most jobs will require at least thirty hours (one year) of credits in a hard science.

The combination of specific classes you take will similarly depend on such factors as degree requirements, your personal choices, the options your school offers, and your eventual goal. For instance, if DNA analysis is your goal, you can concentrate on molecular biology and genetics. Similarly, if toxicology interests you, you would do well to emphasize physical science and chemistry with a particular focus on **pharmacology**.

Many students who are interested in the psychological aspects of forensics aim for a career as a profiler. This is a very specialized field, and only a limited number of positions are available. Nonetheless, if you are interested in following this career path, you might consider taking a double major in psychology and criminal justice, or an undergraduate degree in psychology and a graduate degree in criminology. During your undergraduate years as a psych major, you might also want to take courses in such subjects as crime scene processing and investigation. Don't neglect math, either—a good working knowledge of that subject will be important. Much of your work as a profiler will call for the use of statistics and other mathematical tools.

Specific classes will be somewhat narrowly focused. For example, a class in crime scene evidence gathering will concentrate on the practical tools and procedures used to study and collect information from the scene of a crime. Other individual classes in forensic science you might take will emphasize such topics as the following:

- Anthropology
- Basics of psychology, pathology, and forensic medicine
- Biology
- Digital forensics (computer forensics)
- Evidence reporting
- Fingerprint technology
- Questioned documents

Digital forensics is an increasingly popular and important field of study. As the world in general relies more and more on computers and other digital devices, there is increasing incidence of fraud, embezzlement, and other criminal activities that take advantage of digital technology. Therefore, the field of digital forensics combines several important areas of specialization.

As explained on the website of the Miami/Dade County (Florida) Police Department's Forensic Computer Laboratory, "[F]orensic computer examination is a dynamic science which requires a significant knowledge of multiple disciplines. A balance of computer science, forensics and investigation must be learned to perform competent examinations."

A number of community colleges offer AA degrees in

USING DIGITAL FORENSICS

One case that involved digital forensics was the 2011 trial of Casey Anthony, a Florida woman accused of murdering her young daughter. Investigators found evidence that someone in Anthony's home had conducted an Internet search of information about chloroform three months before the little girl's unexplained disappearance. This was important to the prosecution's case, since it could indicate **premeditated** murder and not spontaneous manslaughter.

However, Anthony and her daughter were living with Anthony's parents at the time, and her own mother claimed that she herself was responsible for the search. Prosecutors challenged this claim, but Anthony's defense team countered by arguing that the forensic analysis had been flawed and so tainted the entire case. When the defendant was acquitted, her lead attorney, José Baez, was quoted by CNN as saying, "[T]he state's computer forensic evidence involving chloroform research, a central element of their premeditation argument, was used to mislead the jury and . . . the flaws in that evidence infected their entire case like a cancer."

Source: "Digital Evidence Discrepancies—Casey Anthony Trial." Browser Forensics, no date, http://www.browserforensics.com/?p=134

digital forensics. One example is Edmonds Community College, Washington (EDCC). Classes in the EDCC program cover such subjects as the legal and ethical aspects of hacking; building **firewall architecture**; **cryptography**; and testing the validity of how evidence to be presented in court was analyzed. Students in the program also have opportunities to work with local law enforcement agencies on ongoing cases.

It's very common for people to enter college without having chosen a major. In some ways, undergraduate school is a chance to sample several subjects and discover the best path for you. Even if you start your university years with a clear focus on forensic science, you'll have a similar chance to look at various subspecialties within the field. This will in turn help you target the area that most interests you, be it digital forensics, blood spatter analysis, toxicology, or another specialty.

Since some positions in forensics require more education than others, your chosen area of study will be a big factor in determining how many years you will be in school. It's perhaps most common for people to earn undergraduate (AA or BS) degrees, typically in two or four years. However, you might want to continue your education further, earning a master of science (MS) or master of science in forensic sciences (MSFS) degree. This typically requires two additional years of study. And you might want to go even further and get a doctor of philosophy (PhD) degree. Each level, of course, will allow you to apply for jobs with progressively higher salaries, greater challenges, and more responsibilities.

Medically related fields of forensics typically require the

BENCH SCIENCE VS. RESEARCH SCIENCE

Simply put, the laboratory aspect of forensic science has two main categories: bench science and research science. The former typically handles the more everyday, routine aspects of research, while the latter focuses on broader issues. One former bench scientist comments:

> Bench science is what you do when you stand (or sit) at a lab bench. You run the experiments that make up the scientific research that is being conducted. It is a very hands-on occupation—with many different timed activities going on simultaneously. I found it sometimes tedious, but never boring.
>
> Bench science is a part of research science. But research science also includes analyzing the data, reading the literature, writing papers, going to meetings, and talking with colleagues. Bench scientists may do all those things as well, but they also spend time conducting the experiments. . . .
>
> My bench was about six feet long (2 m) and I stood in front of it. Think of it like a long durable countertop. It had shelves above it and drawers below it and a couple of kneeholes for sitting on a stool. There were also common benches in each lab, where shared equipment was kept, or where specific procedures were conducted.
>
> When I tried to explain my days to folks who weren't scientists, cooking was the generally understood activity that seemed most like what I did. [Bench science was like] cooking with a different set of tools and a vocabulary that took years to learn, [while] research science is always probing the edges of what is known, maybe developing new recipes, or better understanding old ones.

Source: Anonymous, e-mail to author, July 26, 2011.

most years of study. Medical examiners, pathologists, and forensic psychiatrists need medical degrees. This is, of course, a very long process: typically twelve or thirteen years after high school, including university, medical school, and residency training. Still more education and training may be necessary after that, too. For example, forensic psychiatrists typically get additional education and experience in areas related to legal issues, especially if they are going to work in law enforcement.

AFTER GRADUATING

After you graduate, you will enter an apprenticeship program in your field. Apprenticeship programs are typically paid positions designed to give students serious practical, hands-on experience in a real lab, under the supervision and guidance of working professionals. You'll typically be tested at intervals during the program, and mock trials along the way will help you hone your skills as an expert witness. The number of years you'll spend in an apprenticeship program will depend on a number of factors. Houck comments:

> The length of time for training [in an apprenticeship] varies widely with the discipline and the laboratory. For example, a drug chemist may train for three to six months before taking cases, while a DNA analyst may train for one to two years, and a questioned document examiner may spend up to three years in apprenticeship. In many cases, successfully completing an apprenticeship program is a requirement for the next step in the

process: becoming board certified. Board certification is a series of tests you will have to pass in order to work in a specialized field. Board certification guarantees that professionals in the field who have examined your credentials and evaluated your education and experience have found you to be competent and current in the techniques of your specialty. Board certification is not always required for some jobs in forensic science, such as being a coroner. Nonetheless, in many cases it is unlikely that any organization will hire you for an advanced position if you are not.

When you've completed your apprenticeship program and passed the board exams, it will finally be time to look for a job. There are a number of ways to do this. For one thing, the contacts you have made during your education and apprenticeship may well put you in line for work in a lab where people already know you.

If not, there are plenty of alternatives. A number of websites, especially those of the AAFS and other professional organizations, maintain up-to-date listings of job openings. Also, if you're interested in a job in forensics with the federal government, you can visit the U.S. government's main employment website, www.usajobs.gov, to see what positions are open. Agencies within the Department of Justice, the Department of Homeland Security, and the military are among the government entities that regularly employ forensic scientists.

As you look for work, you might find it helpful to enter potential positions into a spreadsheet. Doing this can make your hunt much easier. You'll be able to rank the various open positions and compare specifics such as requirements, salary and benefits, and location.

REQUIREMENTS FOR SUPPORT JOBS

By no means do all jobs in forensic science require advanced degrees, or even, in some cases, degrees beyond a high school diploma or GED. Some support positions, such as being an assistant or office staff member, require only that you be a high school graduate (or equivalent). Others require a minimum of a two-year AA degree, typically with a year or two of experience or training as well. In some cases, agencies might accept experience and proven expertise in place of formal education.

The salaries, benefits, and responsibilities for support positions are typically lower than for more senior positions. On the other hand, getting a support staff job is a way for you to work in the field of forensics, even if you can't or don't want to go to college. And it can be a start toward moving on to a more senior position.

One example of a support job is identification specialist (sometimes also called

Before you enter the field of forensics, you will receive training from a number of mentors and teachers.

a fingerprint classifier). An assistant to a fingerprint analyst handles the more routine aspects of a fingerprint lab's day-to-day operations, such as cataloging and preserving samples and preparing reports.

The job requirements will differ from agency to agency. For example, some labs require that applicants for an identification specialist opening have a BS degree. On the other hand, in 2011 the Seattle Police Department (SPD) posted an opening for an identification specialist stating that an AA degree in a related field was desired but not required. The SPD further stipulated that applicants

- Be able to process fingerprints from potentially abusive/ threatening people
- Be able to work with bio-hazardous substances such as blood or hazardous chemicals
- Be willing to work rotating shifts and overtime
- Complete coursework in fingerprint science or fingerprint technology, and pass a practical examination on the subject at 80% or higher
- Have a minimum of one year of fingerprinting experience
- Pass a background investigation and physical exam
- Possess a current driver's license

No matter what job you're seeking, when you find an interesting position, it will be time to update your résumé and submit it. If you have a particular company or law enforcement agency in mind, the best route might be to contact the human resources department and ask if you can forward your résumé to one of its representatives. Be sure to ask if there are particular details you should include. It's almost always a good idea to send your information to an organization that interests you, even if no job is available at the moment. Chances are good that the agency will keep your information on file and get in touch when something does become available. (However, it's also good to periodically re-send your résumé to the agency, to make sure you remain on its radar for new jobs.) In addition to your résumé, you may be asked to provide other material as well, such as a personal essay.

If an agency asks you to come in for an interview, be prepared. (This advice, naturally, is true for any job interview.) Practice with friends if you think it will be helpful. Pay attention to your appearance, and be polite and attentive. Don't be discouraged if you are called back several times before a decision is made. For obvious reasons, organizations in the world of law enforcement, such as forensic labs, must be very careful in their hiring choices.

Learning about the possibilities in the field, deciding what to specialize in, studying and training, looking for work, getting hired—all of these are vital steps along the career path you choose. The path can be difficult and sometimes disappointing.

However, you should remember that forensic science is a growing field. It may take a little time, but you're bound to find a job. When you do, you'll typically start in a probationary position. The length of the period will vary from agency to agency—sometimes a few months, sometimes a year. During the probationary period you'll be under the supervision of an experienced employee who will oversee the work you do, making sure that it's up to standard, guiding you as you become more comfortable with the work, and ensuring that you're fitting in well with the overall organization.

Then, when you're ready, your real job will begin.

FOUR

ON THE JOB

THE DAY-TO-DAY, ON-THE-JOB WORK OF A FORENSIC scientist is part of the long chain of activity—gathering evidence, analyzing it, and reporting on the results—that typically follows in the wake of a crime. As a rule, the first forensic specialist to come into play is a crime scene investigator.

Some police forces and other law enforcement agencies use civilian CSIs, that is, investigators who are not part of the regular force. Some of these civilians may be full-time employees but not sworn police officers. Others might be part-time workers who are called in on cases as needed. However, some police departments will train a few sworn officers in CSI techniques. If you are a police officer who is also a CSI, you'll probably spend most of your time on patrol, being called off your regular beat and moving into CSI mode when a detailed investigation of a crime scene is needed.

CRIME SCENE INVESTIGATORS
ON THE JOB

If you're a CSI, a case will usually start for you when you talk to police officers and detectives on the scene of a crime. You'll get an idea of what happened from them and then go to work, observing the scene and collecting evidence. This evidence will then be set aside and preserved, so that it can be taken to a lab for more detailed identification and analysis.

For example, you'll bag small pieces of evidence, being careful to wear latex gloves and use sterile storage containers to avoid contaminating the material collected. A small piece of evidence that might bear an even smaller piece of evidence would be a shell casing to which a few skin cells were clinging, ready to be tested for DNA matching.

When a CSI is processing a crime scene, it is crucial to collect any and all potential evidence.

As you collect evidence, you'll need to judge the importance of each piece. However, at this stage, it will be impossible to know everything that will be important to analysts who will work on the evidence later. So it'll be better to collect too much than too little. Sometimes the evidence you find won't be a physical object that can be carried away, so it will be crucial to observe the entire scene. Ricciuti gives examples:

> Investigators must be aware of everything surrounding them. Are towels in the bathroom wet? Do kitchen odors indicate recent cooking? Is the television on? Are clocks showing the right time? These observations may be unimportant—or they prove to be critical.

CSIs use a number of tools in their work. For example, an offender may have tried to clean up the blood at a crime scene before investigators arrived. This measure typically results in trace evidence only, and what remains may not be easily identifiable as human blood. In that case, you might use a technique involving a chemical such as luminol, which changes color when it comes into contact with blood. Or you might carefully scrape a sample that can be analyzed later.

Some CSI teams are made up of several experts, each of whom focuses on one highly specialized job. For example, one person might concentrate on photographing or drawing diagrams of the scene, while others might collect physical evidence or lift fingerprints. In other instances, such as the CSI department of a small police agency, one person might be responsible for multiple aspects of the job.

One CSI subspecialty is photography. If you become a forensic photographer, you'll be responsible for taking shots of anything that might be relevant to each case. For example, at a murder scene, you might photograph bloodstains on walls, bodies, discarded weapons, or furniture. During an accident investigation, it'll be important to document such evidence as skid marks or damaged factory equipment. You will likely use a number of specialized tools, such as infrared cameras that can pick up images in extremely dark environments.

Later, lab analysts will use your photos to help them in their work. Since in most cases the analysts will not be at the scene themselves, they will need to reconstruct the events of the case in as much detail as possible. So it will be crucial that you provide a complete account of the scene, using close-ups, mid-range shots, and wider shots that allow the analysts to take everything in, as if they were actually at the crime scene. Often, you'll include in the shot a measuring device or token, such as a ruler or a coin, to provide a sense of scale and perspective. And it's likely that you'll work closely with lab analysts at a later date to help them identify details. Your photos might also be used still later in a case, as evidence in a courtroom.

THE EVIDENCE GOES TO A SPECIALIST

When work at the scene is finished, you and your colleagues will deliver the photos, physical evidence, and other materials to a lab. The responsibility then shifts to the specialists who will analyze the particular characteristics of what you've found.

Photographing all parts of a crime scene can provide valuable details to every analyst working on the case.

Of course, where the evidence goes depends on the type of evidence presented. For example, if you are an expert in ballistics and/or toolmarks, then bullets, weapons, and other related items will come your way. The range of evidence you study can be wide. One day you might be looking at a crowbar used to break into a store, and on the next, at photos of holes punched in a wall to see if they match a hammer or a screwdriver used in an assault.

To run your tests, you'll use a battery of instruments. For example, a comparison microscope will let you examine samples side by side. Such a sample might be a bullet taken from a victim's body or a shell casing found nearby. These would then be evaluated against others from guns test-fired for comparison. Using the microscope to examine their surfaces will help you see ballistic "fingerprints" and determine if the evidence was fired from the test gun. Another technique used by firearms specialists involves chemical testing to make serial numbers visible, even though criminals believe they have removed all traces of this identifying information.

Once you've completed your analysis, the next step typically will be to submit a record of your findings to a database such as the one operated by the U.S. Bureau of Alcohol, Tobacco, Firearms, and Explosives (ATF). This database is called the National Integrated Ballistics Information Network (NIBIN).

As of 2011, NIBIN had about 1.6 million entries, which ballistics analysts use in comparing their information against data that has already been filed. If you find a match, you might be able to connect your case with a seemingly unrelated crime. For example, the same weapon used in an assault you're investigating might also have been used in a robbery in another state. According to Sergeant Brandon Huntley, a gun squad supervisor with the Phoenix [Arizona] Police Department, "It [a ballistics database] can help link crime scenes that wouldn't have otherwise been linked together [because] firearms leave markings on the shell casings that are similar to fingerprints or DNA."

FINGERPRINT ANALYSIS

Another familiar part of the forensic process is fingerprint analysis. If this is your specialty, you'll deal with the fingerprint impressions that CSIs have recovered from surfaces at a crime scene. These impressions, caused by tiny amounts of perspiration or body oil, might come from any number of surfaces, including drinking glasses, windows, weapons—even certain types of paper or cardboard.

A variety of sophisticated high-tech equipment is then used to enlarge and highlight prints from the samples collected by CSIs. As in other areas of forensics, new techniques in this field are constantly being developed. For example, new technology can be used to analyze old, partially degraded prints. This means that print analysts can help solve crimes dating back years, the so-called cold cases.

Some forensic scientists specialize in the collection and analysis of fingerprints.

Once you've revealed and recorded a set of prints, you'll compare them against existing files that are already registered in databanks such as the FBI's Automated Fingerprint Identification System (AFIS). If your sampled prints match any that are already on file, the person can be identified with great speed—AFIS can search its files for half a million prints per second.

As a fingerprint specialist, you'll use X rays, lasers, chemical tests, and other high-tech tools to expose and identify prints from these samples—even ones that would otherwise be invisible, such as prints on paper.

Once a fingerprint has been made legible, the usual procedure is to take a digital photo of the evidence, scan the photo into a computer, and store it on a database. In some cases, images are digitally cleaned up to make identification easier. Then you'll examine the tiny details of the prints for "points"—places on the print that, taken together, will be good enough to make a clear match. The more matching points you find, the more reliable the resulting identification will be.

The prints can then be compared against existing files that are already registered in large databases. One such database is the FBI's Integrated Automated Fingerprint Identification System (IAFIS), which stores the records of nearly 100 million people, the majority of whom are previous offenders. These prints are indexed with photos, along with relevant information such as physical characteristics and criminal histories. If your samples match any that are already on file, the suspect can be identified with great speed—IAFIS can complete a search in about half an hour, and sometimes a match is made in as little as ten minutes.

Finally, in what's called verification, a second examiner will look at the evidence and confirm or deny your match. You might use the most sophisticated computer techniques possible, but to minimize the risk of mistakes, a human judge will always have the final say.

DNA ANALYSIS

If you choose a career in another well-known field for identification, DNA analysis, you'll use an array of advanced techniques to examine samples of biological material such as blood, hair, skin, or saliva. The complex identification process

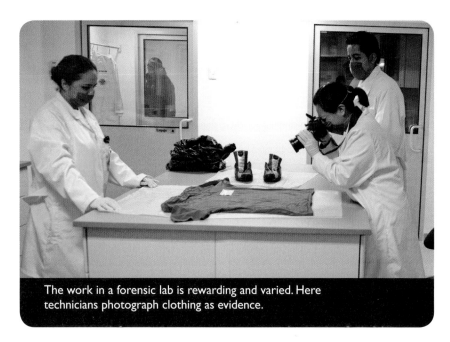

The work in a forensic lab is rewarding and varied. Here technicians photograph clothing as evidence.

typically begins when you use small pieces of synthetic DNA, called probes, that bind to parts of a sample and produce a characteristic pattern. The more probes you use, and the more samples you have, the greater the odds of getting a correct match.

The technology for DNA analysis is improving rapidly. Notably, one early method, restriction fragment length polymorphism (RFLP), needed a sample about the size of a quarter. However, a newer process based on what's called the polymerase chain reaction (PCR) will work with a sample as small as a few skin cells. Furthermore, PCR is less expensive than RFLP, and so is much more accessible to law-enforcement agencies.

Like fingerprint analysts, DNA analysts have access to any

of several far-ranging computer databases. One of these is the FBI's huge Combined DNA Index System (CODIS). All fifty states require law enforcement agencies to send the profiles of certain offenders to CODIS. Regulations in this area have overall become stronger, but they differ from state to state. This means that your responsibilities in terms of compliance will vary depending on your location. For example, New Mexico formerly required law enforcement agencies to send samples to CODIS from convicted felons only. However, in 2006 the state passed legislation known as Katie's Bill, which requires samples from a much larger pool than before: suspects in most felony arrests, in addition to those who are convicted of felonies. The bill is named for Katie Sepich, a college student whose murder remained unsolved for years because her killer's DNA was not on file. The murderer was found years later, however, because after he was convicted of an entirely different crime, his DNA was entered in the database and a match was made.

QUESTIONED-DOCUMENT EXAMINATION AND DIGITAL FORENSICS

Still another branch of forensics is the field of questioned-document examination. Sometimes people who examine questioned documents are incorrectly called "handwriting experts," and part of the document examiner's job is to point out individual differences between one person's writing and another's. Contrary to popular belief, however, a forensic specialist can't tell anything about a person's personality from handwriting samples. There is no documented proof, in fact, that anyone can do this.

If you enter this field, you'll do your detective work with the help of some very specialized instruments like the electrostatic detection apparatus (ESDA). This complex instrument can detect extremely slight impressions left by handwriting, such as a piece of notebook paper that was under another page on which someone had written. Other tools, including chemical testing equipment, infrared cameras, microscopes, and magnifying glasses, will help you carry out such tasks as comparing handwriting, photocopying, or printing samples; examining documents that may have been smudged, altered, or erased; and identifying a specific type of ink or even the work of an individual forger.

Digital forensics experts have a similarly wide range of responsibilities. A typical day in digital forensics might find you recovering deleted e-mails, cracking encrypted text messages or discovering passwords, tracing browser histories, or combing a suspect's computer to retrieve address book entries, files, documents, or images.

Your work might also be to examine a black box recovered from an airline crash, revealing important clues to what caused the disaster. Or you might follow a hacker's path through cyberspace. Furthermore, finding out if a photo has been digitally altered is often part of a day's work. *Scientific American* reporter Hany Farid comments, "Barely a month goes by without some newly uncovered fraudulent image making it into the news."

Criminals are increasingly sophisticated about using digital tools, so forensic experts must constantly come up with new ways to thwart them. David Hoort, a circuit court judge in Michigan, commenting on a seminar he took about cyber-crime, elaborates:

> [I]n drug crimes, if police stop someone . . . the rule of thumb for the criminal is to hide it where the police can't find it. The same is true for computers. There is a great effort to hide child pornography or other evidence of cyber crimes in places that you wouldn't normally look. . . . It's not like the old days where police would go to a criminal down the street and go to the desk or under their bed and [the evidence] is all there.

FORENSIC PSYCHOLOGY
AND PATHOLOGY

Forensic psychology encompasses far more than profiling to get inside the head of a serial killer or sitting down with criminals to find out what makes them tick. For example, forensic psychologists frequently work in prisons, consulting with prison staff on issues such as crisis management or helping inmates come to terms with their mental problems. Or you might be called in on family court cases, such as situations involving child custody.

Another area calling for expertise in forensic psychology is the investigation of a death that focuses on the victim's state of mind. The purpose of this work, which is called a psychological autopsy, is to uncover the cause of death: Murder?

Accident? Suicide? The answer will be important not only to law enforcement officials, but to insurance companies as well. This is because some life insurance policies do not pay if the cause of death is suicide.

If you choose to become a forensic pathologist, you will spend much of your time performing a standard autopsy, looking for evidence on the clothing, skin, bones, and organs of a corpse. Autopsies typically involve such procedures as reviewing medical histories, examining tissue through a microscope, removing and studying organs, and X-raying bodies to detect bullets, broken bones, or other injuries or evidence of foul play. Most of this work is done in a morgue and its laboratory, although sometimes fieldwork is required to gather additional evidence.

EXPERT TESTIMONY

No matter what your specialty is, a major part of your work will be to provide expert testimony in a court case or other legal inquiry. Lawyers on both sides of a trial make frequent use of expert witnesses, who are generally paid for their services. Typically, this will be the last stage of your work on a given case.

Generally speaking, your primary role as an expert witness will be to explain your findings. You'll start by answering questions about your professional credentials, and then go on to state the conclusions you have reached. Often, you'll use visual aids such as animation, photos, or diagrams as part of your testimony. The lawyer who has retained your services will try

FORENSIC ANIMATION

One form of forensics that relies on elements of the creative arts is forensic animation, or the use of the techniques of animation to recreate crime and accident scenes. It combines elements of art with elements of scientific fields such as physics and engineering.

Animations are used during the course of an investigation, but they are particularly valuable in cases that go before a jury. For example, a lawyer might want to demonstrate in court the exact layout of a car accident, along with the precise sequence of events. Animation can re-create scenarios such as what happens when a truck collides with a car. The weight of each vehicle, the speed, and the angle of collision can all be precisely shown.

In such a case, a lawyer would likely commission an animated simulation. Combined with an expert's testimony, the animation will give judges and juries a clear understanding of an event that might otherwise be hard to visualize. The use of this visual aid has been controversial, since animations are obviously re-creations of events rather than the events themselves. Nonetheless, they can be useful. Software engineer Dean Ballard, whose career has included work in a company that produced forensic animations, describes the work:

> What our company . . . did was produce short animations of scenes for liability lawsuits. We would work with an expert witness to create animated graphics that would help the expert explain the case to a judge or jury.
>
> The most common example of our work was an animation of a traffic accident. We would get an approximate description of the shape of the cars involved, and all of the relevant details of the scene, in terms of coordinate geometry. The expert witness would also work out the motion of the cars through time, again in coordinate geometry.
>
> We would enter all of that data into a control file, then our program would use that data to calculate, frame by frame, a short animated movie of the accident that could be displayed on a computer. The most interesting part for me was writing the program that would read in the raw data, calculate 3-D projections for each frame (including the always-tricky hidden line removal algorithm), and assemble them into an animation file.
>
> The intention was that an animation could be shown to a judge or jury, providing a real-time, or slow motion, look at what happened, and give them a better idea of the whole event than they would get from a verbal description or still images. In practice almost all of these cases were settled out of court, so I don't think any of my work ever made it to the courtroom.

Source: e-mail to author, August 11, 2011

to put you and your opinions in the best possible light, asking questions designed to favor the defense or prosecution. The opposition will do its best to discredit you professionally and to question your opinions by seeking to show weaknesses in your methods and conclusions.

This is where your ability to think rationally, communicate clearly, and stay cool will be put to the test. The jury and judge must be able to understand the circumstances of the case and what your findings mean to prove, or disprove. This is not simple. One expert, quoted by Connie Fletcher in *Every Contact Leaves a Trace*, comments, "Forensic scientists and technical experts have to be able to go into a courtroom, articulate [speak clearly] their findings, think on their feet, be fair, be objective, be unbiased and withstand the vitriol [antagonism] of defense attorneys. That's a pretty tall order."

SUPPORT STAFF

Of course, you might follow a career path that takes you (at least at first) not into a forensic specialty but into the support staff of experts. In this case, you can choose from a wide array of possibilities. Private labs and forensics departments of law enforcement agencies have need of people who can fill such positions as information technology (IT) experts, polygraph examiners, artists, X-ray technicians, and even divers who specialize in recovering submerged evidence. Furthermore, heightened concern over environmental issues has created a number of new positions combining environmental studies with forensics. For example, laboratories often need techni-

As a forensic scientist, you will probably be called to testify in court cases, like Dr. Henry Lee did in the O.J. Simpson trial.

cians to handle the disposal of hazardous waste.

One typical support job is that of crime lab assistant (CLA). CLAs work in labs and at crime scenes, assisting CSIs and other professionals. A CLA's typical duties include collecting, cataloging, testing, and storing evidence; operating and maintaining lab equipment, preparing reports and keeping records, and testifying in court.

Another support position is that of fingerprint classifier (sometimes also called a fingerprint examiner or identification specialist). If you work in this job, your day will include such tasks as enhancing photographs of fingerprints, comparing prints taken from crime scenes against existing records, and taking the fingerprints of corpses or suspects.

Or you might take on another important support job:

crime scene technician (also known as forensic science investigator or field evidence technician). Essentially, this position consists of acting as the assistant to a crime scene investigator. As a crime scene technician, your daily responsibilities might include making impressions of shoeprint or tire tracks, or cataloging and securing evidence.

Whether you are a support technician or working in another capacity, there are many rewards to being part of a forensic science team. You'll have the satisfaction of a challenging job. You'll know that you are part of a body of professionals who are helping to protect their communities from harm. Of course, these are not the only rewards you'll receive. No one can live on good feelings alone. As in any field, a career in forensic science will also give you concrete rewards—that is, compensation in the form of salaries and benefits.

BENEFITS AND SALARIES

A CAREER IN FORENSIC SCIENCE CAN BE A SOURCE of great satisfaction for you. For one thing, you'll be pursuing science in a fast-paced setting that uses cutting-edge technology. You'll be working on an array of challenging and varied projects. You'll be doing something that makes the world a better place. On top of all that, the job market is strong and the field can pay well. As the website of the Forensic Sciences Foundation notes, "Essentially every branch of forensic science offers opportunity for personal growth, career advancement, and increasing financial compensation."

Broadly speaking, employment prospects in forensic science are good, and it's estimated that this will remain true. Although the nation's overall crime rates are regrettably high, this bad situation is balanced by the favorable employment picture: there are many job opportunities in forensics (and in other areas of law enforcement, for that matter).

The U.S. Bureau of Labor Statistics (BLS) estimates that the number of full-time forensic scientists in this country will increase by at least 20 percent, and perhaps by as much as 30 percent, by 2018. This is faster than the average growth in the overall U.S. workforce. Even if growth is not this quick—and estimates vary considerably—the market for jobs in forensics is expected to remain strong. A website devoted to career opportunities and maintained by Indiana University and Purdue University makes the following prediction: "Jobs for forensic science technicians are expected to increase much faster than average through 2016."

Perhaps the biggest single market in the near future will be in digital forensics. This was once a small part of the over-

With new technological advances and evolving investigation techniques, forensic science will remain a growing job market for years.

all information technology field. Today, however, thanks to exploding Internet and cell phone use, new worlds have opened up for cybercriminals. Offenders run the gamut from petty thieves to high-level embezzlers. Reporter Cecilia Capuzzi Simon of *The New York Times*, who has investigated the trend, notes that virtually all offenders use some kind of digital device: "It is the rare criminal who doesn't leave a digital trail."

Efforts to stop cybercrime have struggled to keep pace. For example, the number of regional computer forensics labs that the FBI operates shot from three in 2003 to sixteen in 2011. Also in 2011 the FBI employed approximately 500 staff at its main lab in Virginia, plus a total of about 250 more in its regional labs. These facilities were handling more than one million cases per year, and the numbers will no doubt increase as time goes on.

FACTORS IN EMPLOYMENT

As is true with most full-time jobs, compensation (that is, the salary and benefits package) for a career worker in the forensic sciences will generally be good. The pay range and benefits can vary quite a bit, however. One of the most important factors will be the amount of related education, training, and experience you have. Someone with an advanced degree or years of experience will be preferred over someone who is less educated or less experienced. The pay level at which you start, and your chances for promotion, will also be better if you have significant experience and education.

Another factor in determining your salary will be the organization for which you work. The vast majority of forensic scientists work in law enforcement at the city, county, state, or federal level. Nonfederal law enforcement agencies include police departments, sheriff's offices, district attorney's offices, and medical examiner's offices.

Among the many federal agencies that have forensic specialists on staff, for example, are the following:

- Bureau of Alcohol, Tobacco, Firearms, and Explosives (ATF)
- Central Intelligence Agency (CIA)
- Department of Justice (DOJ)
- Drug Enforcement Administration (DEA)
- Federal Bureau of Identification (FBI)
- The branches of the military (Army, Navy, Marines, Air Force, and Coast Guard)
- U.S. Secret Service (USSS)

On the other hand, you might choose to work in the private sector. Some larger organizations, such as medical labs, insurance companies, and engineering firms, need full- or part-time forensic scientists. Alternatively, you might prefer to work for yourself on a freelance basis, or for a private company that consults or does analytical work (such as DNA analysis or drug testing) for law enforcement agencies and other companies. These smaller organizations typically don't have their own full-time forensic analysts, and so rely on the on-call help of expert subcontractors.

Another employment option in forensics is to return to a college setting and become a professor teaching the next generation of forensic scientists.

And some forensic scientists work in academia—that is, the world of higher learning. For example, you might choose to be a professor at a university or community college doing research and teaching while occasionally consulting with law enforcement agencies. This is typically the case in highly specialized fields such as forensic anthropology, since few law enforcement agencies need full-time scientists in such positions.

Of course, the amount of time you work will also be a factor in how much you earn. Some forensic scientists are on salary and work more or less normal forty-hour weeks (although they may be eligible for extra pay for overtime or working odd hours). Meanwhile, private firms or individuals who are on call and paid hourly might work more or fewer hours, depending on circumstances.

A less important factor in determining your salary and benefits is where you live. Broadly speaking, compensation for forensic scientists tends to be somewhat lower in the southern United States than elsewhere in the country. On the other hand, the overall number of forensic specialists in a given area doesn't necessarily match its pay scales. For example, on a statewide basis in 2011 the largest numbers of forensic scientists were in Arizona and Florida, but those in Wisconsin and Massachusetts earned the most.

Seniority—that is, the number of years you have been working—is also a factor. The more senior a position is, the greater the responsibility and pay, with the senior manager of a forensic lab receiving significantly more than an entry-level employee. Linked to the question of promotion is the quality of your performance evaluations. Performance evaluations are "report cards" that are made on a regular basis by your superiors within the organization. They judge how well you are doing your work and determine if your performance evaluation warrants a step up in seniority and the increase in pay that comes with it.

As an example of how seniority works, state agencies in California usually hire forensic scientists at a government-set entry level called Criminalist I. You then have the opportunity to be promoted to more a senior position at the Criminalist II level. A further advance, to the Criminalist III level, typically will put you in a management position, supervising groups within a lab or department. The next promotional step is to crime laboratory director, with responsibilities for planning, organizing, and directing the operations of an entire lab.

BENEFITS

A good salary is not the only incentive that companies typically offer to their employees. Benefits are also an important part of any compensation package.

Typically, part-time employees are not eligible for complete benefits packages. As with any job, part-time work is paid by the hour, with benefits added if you work a certain number of hours per week. Again, this varies. Some companies offer benefits to employees who work just three-quarters or even half time.

Perhaps the most important single benefit for any employee is medical and/or dental insurance, both for individuals and their families. But there are many other advantages, including paid and unpaid vacation, holidays, sick leave, and retirement plans. Others include life insurance plans, savings plans, and reimbursements for travel expenses.

Furthermore, companies and organizations typically have programs to help employees if they are injured or seriously ill, or if they need a period of time away from work for some reason. For example, your company might let you take up to twelve weeks of unpaid leave in the event of the birth of a child or a personal health problem.

Related to this is a system that many organizations offer, called voluntary leave transfer. Under this program, employees can donate unused days off to other employees who have used all their allotted days off. This system can be extremely important to employees who need additional time to recover from an illness or to care for a family member.

Another benefit that is commonly part of the package reflects a practice of many agencies, namely, to encourage employees to continue their education. For example, a company might pay for an employee to attend professional classes. It might also give the employee days off to conduct research that is related to his or her work. And organizations typically require their employees to go through periodic refresher courses and seminars to keep them up to date on new techniques. Time off and expenses, including tuition, are typically covered in such cases.

The skills and knowledge you'll pick up through this type of continuing education will serve several purposes.

Your education and training usually does not end once you get a job in forensics. Most companies or organizations will help you pay for additional classes to keep you informed of the latest developments in your field or specialty.

Not only is it personally fulfilling, it will help you get better at your job. If you are better at your job, then the agency you work for obviously benefits as well. Furthermore, getting better at your job is an excellent path to promotion into higher, more prestigious, and more satisfying positions for yourself.

GENERAL SALARY RANGES

Pay scales and benefits generally differ depending on whether you work in the private sector or in a government agency. As a general rule, jobs in the private sector for forensic scientists are higher paid than those for equivalent government jobs. However, benefits packages may not be as comprehensive as in the government. More specific comparisons are hard to make because private companies are reluctant to state the compensation ranges they offer and generally do not post them, even on their individual websites.

In the case of a federal agency like the Department of Justice or the FBI, your pay will depend on guidelines that determine the salaries of all federal employees. These guidelines form a plan known as the General Schedule (GS). The GS has fifteen pay grades, and there are ten steps within each grade. For each grade and each step, there is a specified salary level.

In government, as in the private sector, the salary differences between entry-level positions and those requiring more training and experience are great. For example, if you had just started in the workforce in 2011, you could expect to earn about $22,000 as an entry-level technician. With some associated previous experience, however, you could expect to start the same job at a higher salary, about $36,000.

In the middle range, those with expertise in a specialty, such as latent print analysis, could expect to earn an average of about $47,000. And for more senior scientists, the pay was in the $96,000 range.

In any event, the high demand for digital forensics experts means that salaries in this field are higher than average. In a 2011 article in the British newspaper *The Guardian*, cyber-security expert Piers Wilson wrote, "Today, cyber security is a rapidly growing global issue and an ever increasing market." Depending on experience, as of 2011 people in this field could expect to earn $50,000 to $100,000—or even more.

Pay scales for other positions, including support jobs, differ widely. For example, in 2011, the police department in Bryan, Texas, listed a position as a crime scene unit supervisor. The annual salary range for starting this job was about $42,000 to $46,500 per year, depending on experience. A full range of benefits was included in the compensation package, as is generally true for any other full-time job.

As of 2011 a fingerprint classifier for the state of California could expect a starting salary in the range of $27,000 to $42,000. In contrast, a roughly equivalent job with the FBI had a pay range of about $26,000 to $36,000 per year.

Another example of a salary range for a forensics expert is a job opening posted in 2011 by the Valdosta [Georgia] Police

Department. This job was for a forensic firearms specialist. The range for someone starting in this position was about $39,500 to $53,000. A DNA scientist for the Orange County Police Department in California (in the classification "Forensic Scientist I," which is not a supervisory position) would in 2011 have earned between $54,000 and $72,700.

Some agencies calculate the salaries for some positions on an hourly basis. For example, in 2011 the Seattle Police Department posted a job opening for an identification technician. The salary range was $26 to $30 per hour depending on experience and education. If the successful applicant worked forty hours a week, that would be a yearly salary of approximately $50,000 to $58,000.

Of course, the salary and benefits you can earn will change over time, so it's important to get up-to-date information. Internet sources with listings of current job openings, such as the AAFS site, will give you an accurate idea of salary ranges.

Forensic scientists who work on call typically bill by the hour. These hourly rates are generally very high, making up for the lack of steady paychecks and benefits of a full-time salaried job. For example, Elkins comments about consulting forensic anthropologists: "Their fees vary all over the place, but $100 to $200 an hour would cover most of them. If they wind up expert-witnessing in court, the fees can go way up. At the same time, I can't recall a single case where a request from a law enforcement agency was turned down because there was no money to cover a fee."

As you explore a career in forensic science, it will become increasingly clear that you will have a broad range of choices. You can go into any number of specialized fields. You can work full time or part time. You can find a niche in the private sector, in academia, or in government. No matter what combination you choose, your job will be tough and demanding—but also challenging and rewarding.

GLOSSARY

accredited school—A school that is recognized, typically by a professional organization and/or a regional educational authority, as meeting minimum educational standards.

autopsy—A medical examination of a corpse to determine the cause of death.

chain of custody—The record of the "trail" of evidence beginning at the time each item is collected. Typically this involves the transfer to one or more labs, storage, and so on.

corruption—Illegal conduct by someone in power, typically involving bribery.

criminology—The scientific study of crime.

cryptography—The science of studying codes. In the forensic sciences, this usually means deciphering, or writing and solving this type of system.

firewall architecture—The process of creating security systems for computer networks.

lay public—The general public, not experts or professionals in a particular field.

morgue—A storage and examination facility for corpses, typically maintained by a law enforcement agency.

pharmacology—The study of drugs.

polygraph examination—A means of generating a record that will enable analysts to evaluate the truthfulness of a person's responses to questions.

premeditated—Thought out ahead of time. For example, a premeditated murder is one that was planned, not spontaneous.

testimony—The verbal statement given by a witness in a court of law, under oath.

trace evidence—Tiny bits of evidence, such as paint chips, discovered at the scene of a crime.

white-collar crimes—Crimes that are carried out by people typically involved in business enterprises or computer technology. Examples are embezzlement, fraud, swindles, and insider trading.

NOTES

INTRODUCTION

p. 8: "An assailant may unknowingly carry . . . ": Jennifer Viegas, "Cat fur puts criminals behind bars," *Discovery News*, MSNBC, www.msnbc.msn.com/id/35948243/ns/technology_and_science-science/t/cat-fur-puts-criminals-behind-bars/

p. 8-9: "Forensics is not about one body . . . ": Edward Ricciuti, *Science 101: Forensics* (New York: HarperCollins, 2007), 1.

p. 10-11: "Forensic science databases…": Mara Stine, "CSI vs. Real Life," *Portland (OR) Tribune*, November 14, 2008, http://www.portlandtribune.com/news/story.php?story_id=122671590561640000

p. 12-13: "The sole objective . . . ": Henry C. Lee, *Cracking Cases* (Amherst, NY: Prometheus, 2002), 18.

CHAPTER 1: THE BIG PICTURE

p. 14: "Overall, today's rapidly advancing forensic technology . . .": Lee, *Cracking Cases*, 13.

p. 16: "Only in the last century": Max M. Houck, *Science vs. Crime* (New York: Facts on File, 2009), xii.

p. 17: "It may seem odd" Houck, *Science vs. Crime*, 2.

p. 19: "[T]he most difficult things to collect . . . ": Fletcher, *Every Contact Leaves a Trace*, 41.

p. 19: "Physical evidence may be": Anonymous, "Criminalistics: Scope of Work," *Forensic Sciences Foundation*, www.forensicsciencesfoundation.org/career_paths/criminalistics2.htm

p. 22: "The patterns of bloodstains . . . ": Ricciuti, *Science 101: Forensics*, 26.

p. 28: "A pile of bones found in the basement . . . ": Ricciuti, *Science 101: Forensics*, 74.

p. 29, 30: "The only full-time [practitioners] I know about . . .": Aaron Elkins, e-mail to author, August 16, 2011.

CHAPTER 2: WHAT IT TAKES

p. 41: "You have to be very adaptive . . . ": Fletcher, *Every Contact Leaves a Trace*, 20.

p. 46: "Since the program": Natalie Angier, "A Hit in School, Maggots and All," *The New York Times*, May 11, 2009, www.nytimes.com/2009/05/12/science/12angi.html?pagewanted=all

p. 46: "I love this class! . . . ": Angier, "A Hit in School, Maggots and All," *The New York Times*, May 11, 2009.

p. 48: "Becoming involved in activities . . . ": Laura Sheahan, "Stepping Away From the Bench: Science Policy at the National Academies," *Science*, February 7, 2003, http:// sciencecareers.sciencemag.org/career_development/ previous_issues/articles/2170/stepping_away_from_the_ bench_science_policy_at_the_national_academies

p. 49: "dedicated to the education . . . ": Anonymous, "Welcome," *Young Forensic Scientists Forum*, www2.aafs.org/ yfsf/

CHAPTER 3: HIGHER EDUCATION
AND TRAINING

p. 53: "If the job market . . . ": Dale Nute, "Advice about a Career in Forensic Science," www.criminology.fsu.edu/ faculty/nute/FScareers.html

p. 59: "[F]orensic computer examination is a . . . ": Anonymous, "Forensic Computer Laboratory." *Miami-Dade Police Department website*, www.miamidade.gov/mdpd/ fcls.asp

p. 63: "The length of time . . . ": Houck, *Science vs. Crime*, 17.

CHAPTER 4: ON THE JOB

p. 71: "Investigators must be aware . . . ": Ricciuti, *Science 101: Forensics*, 23.

p. 74: "It [a ballistics database] can help . . . ": Michael Ferraresi, "Phoenix crime-gun database could expand to other Valley cities," *Arizona Republic*, May 10, 2010, www.

azcentral.com/community/ahwatukee/articles/2010/05/1
0/20100510phoenix-gun-crime-database.\

p. 79: "Barely a month goes by . . . ": Hany Farid, "Digital
Forensics: How Experts Uncover Doctored Images," *Scientific American*, June 2, 2008, www.scientificamerican.
com/article.cfm?id=digital-image-forensics

p. 80: "[I]n drug crimes . . . ": Quoted in Jon Szerlag,
"Mastering computer forensics: Judge Hoort gains
technological insight," Ionia County (MI) *Sentinel-Standard*, August 3, 2011, Sentinel-standard.com,
www.sentinel-standard.com/features/x242973918/
Hoort-gets-trained-in-computer-forensics

p. 84: "Forensic scientists and technical experts . . . ": Quoted
in Fletcher, *Every Contact Leaves a Trace*, 323.

CHAPTER 5: SALARIES AND BENEFITS

p. 87: "Essentially every branch of forensic science . . . ":
Anonymous, "How Much Money Will I Make?" *Career
Paths*, Forensic Sciences Foundation, www.forensic-sciencesfoundation.org/career_paths/fs_compensation.
htm

p. 88: "Jobs for forensic science technicians . . . ": Anonymous,
"Major Career Connections: Major Profile: Forensic &
Investigative Sciences (IRC)," *Indiana University/Purdue
University*, http://uc.iupui.edu/uploadedFiles/Major_
Career_Connections/Forensic.pdf

p. 96: "Today, cyber security . . ." Piers Wilson, "Behind the
Job Title: Cyber Security Consultant," *The Guardian*

(U.K.), February 8, 2011, http://careers.guardian.co.uk/working-in-cyber-security

p. 97: "Their fees vary all over the place . . . ": Elkins, e-mail to author, August 21, 2011.

FURTHER INFORMATION

Parks, Peggy J. *DNA Evidence and Investigation*. San Diego, CA: Reference Point, 2011.

Stefoff, Rebecca, *Forensic Science Investigated: Crime Labs*. New York: Marshall Cavendish, 2011.

WEBSITES

American Academy of Forensic Sciences

The website of the largest association of forensic science professionals.

www.aafs.org

American Forensic Association

This is the website of a prominent organization supporting research and other aspects of forensic science.

www.americanforensics.org

Crime Scene Investigator Network

A good source of information about CSI.

www.crime-scene-investigator.net/index.html

Forensics Illustrated

A comprehensive site of information gathered by a high school teacher of forensic science.

www.bsapp.com/forensics_illustrated/

"Forensic Science"

A website with excellent information, created by students. http://library.thinkquest.org/04oct/00206/index1.htm.

Forensic Sciences Foundation

Brief introductions to various fields, and other information. http://fsf.aafs.org/career_paths/what-forensic-science

Forensicscience.net

Learn more about what it takes to become a forensic scientist including the required education, roles and responsibilities, best places to work, and expected salaries. www.forensicscience.net

BIBLIOGRAPHY

BOOKS

Brown, Pat. *The Profiler*. Farmington Hills, MI: Voice, 2010.

Englert, Rod. *Blood Secrets: Chronicles of a Crime Scene Reconstructionist*. New York: St. Martin's Press, 2010.

Fletcher, Connie. *Every Contact Leaves a Trace*. New York: St. Martin's Press, 2006.

Kollman, Dana. *Never Suck a Dead Man's Hand: Curious Adventures of a CSI*. Seattle, WA: Kensington, 2007.

Lee, Henry C. *Cracking Cases*. Amherst, NY: Prometheus, 2002.

Ricciuti, Edward. *Science 101: Forensics*. New York: Harper-Collins, 2007.

PERIODICALS

Albert, A. Midori. "Education and Career Planning Recommendations," *UNCW Forensic Anthropology*, http://people.uncw.edu/albertm/job.htm

Angier, Natalie. "A Hit in School, Maggots and All," *New York Times*, May 11, 2009. www.nytimes.com/2009/05/12/science/12angi.html?pagewanted=all.

Farid, Hany. "Digital Forensics: How Experts Uncover Doctored Images," *Scientific American*, June 2, 2008, www.scientificamerican.com/article.cfm?id=digital-image-forensics

Ferraresi, Michael. "Phoenix crime-gun database could expand to other Valley cities," *Arizona Republic*, May 10, 2010, www.azcentral.com/community/ahwatukee/articles/2010/05/10/20100510phoenix-gun-crime-database

"Major Career Connections: Major Profile: Forensic & Investigative Sciences (IRC)," *Indiana University/Purdue University*, http://uc.iupui.edu/uploadedFiles/Major_Career_Connections/Forensic.pdf

Mauro, Marisa. "Take All Prisoners: What Is Forensic Psychology?" *Psychology Today*, June 7, 2010, www.psychologytoday.com/blog/take-all-prisoners/201006/what-is-forensic-psychology

Sheahan, Laura. "Stepping Away From the Bench: Science Policy at the National Academies," *Science*, February 7, 2003, http://sciencecareers.sciencemag.org/

career_development/previous_issues/articles/2170/
stepping_away_from_the_bench_science_policy_at_the_
national_academies

Simon, Cecilia Capuzzi. "So You Want to Be a Cybersleuth?"
New York Times, December 26, 2006. www.nytimes.
com/2009/01/04/education/edlife/continuinged-t.html.

"Career Switching? Elementary, My Dear Watson,"
New York Times, December 26, 2008. www.nytimes.
com/2009/01/04/education/edlife/continuingedbox-t.
html

Stine, Mara. "CSI vs. Real Life," *Portland (OR) Tribune*,
November 14, 2008. http://www.portlandtribune.com/
news/story.php?story_id=122671590561640000.

Szerlag, Jon. "Mastering computer forensics: Judge Hoort
gains technological insight," *Ionia County (MI) Sentinel-Standard*, August 3, 2011. Sentinel-standard.com,
www.sentinel-standard.com/features/x242973918/
Hoort-gets-trained-in-computer-forensics.

Viegas, Jennifer. "Cat Fur Puts Criminals Behind Bars,"
Discovery News, MSNBC, www.msnbc.msn.com/
id/35948243/ns/technology_and_science-science/t/
cat-fur-puts-criminals-behind-bars/

Wilson, Piers. "Behind the Job Title: Cyber Security Consultant," *The Guardian* (U.K.), February 8, 2011, http://
careers.guardian.co.uk/working-in-cyber-security

INDEX

INDEX

ABOUT THE AUTHOR

ADAM WOOG is the author of many books for adults, young adults, and children. His most recent books are *Military Might and Global Intervention* in the Controversy! series, and the five other titles in this series. Woog lives in his hometown of Seattle, Washington, with his wife. Their daughter, a college student, is majoring in criminal justice and criminology.